This is Lebanon...
Famous Lebanese

هيدا لبنان...
مشاهير لبنان

lingualism

ISBN: 978-1-962752-20-6

Written by Sarah Khoury and Matthew Aldrich

Edited by Charbel Ghaleb and Matthew Aldrich

Audio by Ayman Sayegh

website: www.lingualism.com

email: contact@lingualism.com

TABLE OF CONTENTS

INTRODUCTION

This book is the first in the (forthcoming) series هيدا لبنان (*This is Lebanon...*). Book One, مشاهير لبنان (*Famous Lebanese*) presents **twelve units**, each focusing on a significant figure who has shaped, or continues to shape, Lebanon's cultural, political, or social life.

The texts are written entirely in Lebanese Arabic at an **advanced level** (C1–C2), making them suitable for learners who have studied Lingualism's intermediate-level materials and are ready to push their language skills further. The writing style is clear yet sophisticated, offering learners an authentic challenge while staying accessible with support materials.

Each of the twelve units is built around a central text and is accompanied by:

- **Pre-reading questions** to activate background knowledge and spark curiosity

- **Key vocabulary** drawn from the text to support comprehension

- **Comprehension questions** to check understanding of details and main ideas

- **Discussion and essay prompts** to encourage critical thinking and deeper engagement

- **Professional audio recordings** of each text read by a native speaker from Beirut, to support listening practice and reinforce natural pronunciation and rhythm

Together, these features make the book not only a reading resource but also a complete toolkit for learners aiming to achieve a high level of proficiency in Levantine Arabic.

HOW TO USE THIS BOOK

This book is designed to help you get the most out of your studies as you advance into the highest levels of Lebanese Arabic. To benefit fully, it's important to approach each unit actively and strategically. The following guide explains the steps you can take to make the most of the materials provided.

Unit Introductions and Pre-Reading Questions

Each unit begins with a short introduction in English. This introduction gives you some background about the person featured in the text. Having this context before you begin reading in Arabic helps activate your prior knowledge, set expectations, and make it easier to make educated guesses as you encounter new vocabulary and expressions.

The **Pre-Reading Questions** are designed to get you thinking about the subject. Try answering them in Lebanese Arabic, either by speaking out loud or writing your answers. If you are studying with a tutor or in a class, these questions can spark discussion. If you are studying on your own, they are still valuable to prepare your mind to notice key concepts and vocabulary when you read the text.

Vocabulary Exercise

Each unit highlights **10 Key Vocabulary items** from the text. These are words or phrases you will see in **bold** within the text (or underlined in a section title). Before reading, you are given their definitions in Arabic—but without the actual words themselves.

Your task is to match each definition to the correct word or phrase from the text. This activity forces you to pay close attention to both the definitions and the surrounding context in the text itself. Use clues from the sentences to help you decide which word matches which definition.

If you are studying with a teacher, you can work together to discuss possible matches before checking the answers. If you are studying alone, try to complete the activity on your own first, then check your answers using the **answer key** at the back of the book.

Approaching the Reading Text

The main text of each unit is a challenging article written in Lebanese Arabic. There are few vowel markings (tashkeel), just as you would see in authentic native materials. This means you must rely on your vocabulary knowledge, grammar skills, and context to determine the correct pronunciation and meaning.

There are many ways you can approach the text. Experiment with different methods to see what works best for you:

- **Listening First**: Play the audio without looking at the text. See how much you can understand by ear alone. Then listen again after studying the text to measure your progress.

- **Reading While Listening**: Follow along in the text while the narrator reads at a natural, native speed. Don't pause—just let yourself absorb as much as you can.

- **Reading Alone**: Read the text without audio, at your own pace. Focus on meaning, guess unknown words from context, and mark phrases you find difficult.

- **Checking with Audio**: Listen again while reading, and this time mark tashkeel only on words you were unsure of. Use the audio as a tool to confirm or correct your guesses.

The English translations are included at the back of the book—not beside the Arabic text. This is intentional. At this level, you should try to understand the text without relying too quickly on translations. Use them only when you are truly stuck.

Using the Audio

The recordings are available as a **free download from our website** and also to **stream on our YouTube channel**. The narrator speaks at a natural, conversational speed—faster than the recordings in our intermediate materials.

This is meant to challenge your listening comprehension at an advanced level. That said, if needed, you can slow down playback on YouTube. You can also repeat short sections of the audio to practice shadowing—reading the text out loud while trying to match the speaker's pronunciation, intonation, and rhythm.

Visit **www.lingualism.com/audio**, where you can find the free accompanying audio to download or stream (at variable playback rates).

Comprehension Questions

After the text, you will find **10 comprehension questions**. These test your understanding of the details, main ideas, and implications in the text. Try to answer them in Arabic if you can.

- **On your own**: Write your answers in a notebook. Check back in the text to confirm, but avoid relying too much on the translation.

- **With a tutor or class**: Discuss your answers aloud. Let the questions guide you back into the text to justify your ideas.

Discussion and Essay Prompts

Finally, each unit includes open-ended questions designed for deeper reflection and critical thinking. These questions are not about right or wrong answers; they are meant to help you **express your opinions and ideas in Arabic**.

If you are studying independently, treat them as writing prompts. Write short essays or journal entries in Lebanese Arabic. If you are studying with a tutor, use them as conversation starters. They are especially useful for building fluency and practicing expressing complex ideas naturally.

Final Tip

There is no single "correct" path through a unit. Some learners prefer to listen first, then read. Others read first, then listen. The important thing is to challenge yourself, stay engaged, and use the different components—text, audio, vocabulary, and questions—in ways that push you beyond your comfort zone while still being manageable.

Above all, enjoy the journey. As you read about these remarkable Lebanese figures, you are not only improving your Arabic but also gaining insight into the history, culture, and voices that shape Lebanon today. By the time you complete this book, you will not only have strengthened your command of Levantine Arabic, but also prepared yourself to approach the wider series with confidence, curiosity, and a deeper connection to the language.

فيروز

Fairuz is one of the most beloved voices in the Arab world and a symbol of Lebanese cultural identity. Her songs, filled with emotion and simplicity, became a soundtrack for generations, accompanying people through moments of hope, longing, and daily life. From the streets of Beirut to international stages, Fairuz brought a unique blend of poetry and melody that touched listeners across borders. Even today, her voice remains a unifying thread in Lebanon's story, reminding people of beauty, resilience, and shared memory.

Pre-Reading Questions

1.   بتتوقع إنو الطفولة الصعبة بتقوّي شخصية الفنان؟ ليش أو لأ؟

2.   بتعرف شي عن الأخوين رحباني وشغلن مع فيروز؟

3.   برأيك، ليش بعض الأصوات بتضل بالذاكرة حتى بعد مرور أجيال؟

Vocabulary

Below are ten definitions. Each one matches a word or phrase that appears in bold in the reading text (or underlined in a section title).

Before reading, try to understand each definition and think of what Arabic term might fit.

Then, as you read, look for the bold words and phrases in the text. Use the surrounding context to help you match them to the definitions.

An answer key is provided at the back of the book.

1. ابتعاد عن الخلافات بدون ما تدخل
2. جو فيه عاطفة وراحة
3. حدث بيغيّر مجرى حياة الشخص
4. شي بيريّح النفس وبيعطي أمان
5. شي معنوي أو فني بيضل بعد غياب الشخص
6. عواميد قديمة موجودة بالمواقع الأثرية
7. غنى فيه مبالغة ليفرجي القدرات
8. مجموعة أفكار وأساليب بتشكّل هوية فنية واضحة
9. مجموعة بتغنّي سوا بنفس الوقت
10. هيبة ورصانة بطريقة التصرف

فيروز: الصوت اللي جمع لبنان والعالم العربي

الطفولة والبداية

فيروز اسما الحقيقي نهاد حدّاد. خلقت سنة ١٩٣٥ بحيّ زقاق البلاط ببيروت. الحي كان بسيط، بيوت قديمة، ناس بتعرف بعضا، وولاد بيلعبوا بالشارع من الصبح للمسا. عيلتا كانت من الطبقة المتواضعة، وبيّا كان موظّف بالمطبعة التابعة لجرنال لبناني. جوّ العيلة كان هادي، بس مليان **محبة ودفا**. من هي وصغيرة، كان صوتا يلفت اللي حواليا، لأنو نضيف، واضح، وفي شي بيلمس من أول لحظة.

بفترة الحرب العالمية التانية، الراديو كان وسيلة التسلية الأساسية عند الناس. فيروز كانت تقعد تسمع الأغاني القديمة، خصوصاً أسمهان وليلى مراد، وتتخيّل حالا على المسرح. بالمدرسة، كانت تشارك **بالكورال**، والمعلّمين لاحظوا إنو صوتا مميز عن باقي الولاد والبنات.

من الإذاعة إلى الأخوين رحباني

بعمر الستعش، سمعا حليم الرومي، مدير الإذاعة اللبنانية بوقتا، وقرر يعطيا فرصة. هو اللي سمّا فيروز، لأنو صوتا بنظرو كان متل الحجر الكريم. بالإذاعة، بلّشت تغنّي أغاني قصيرة وخفيفة، وبسرعة صار إلا جمهور صغير عم يكبر يوم عن يوم.

سنة ١٩٥١، تعرّفت على الأخوين رحباني، عاصي ومنصور، وكان هاللقاء **نقطة تحول** بحياتا الفنية. عاصي شاف فيا الصوت اللي بيقدر يحمل مشروع موسيقي جديد للبنان. من هون، وْلِدَت الشراكة اللي صارت من أشهر الشراكات بتاريخ الموسيقى العربية. مع الوقت، اتزوجت فيروز من عاصي، وصاروا هالتلاتة يشكلوا **مدرسة فنية كاملة**.

المهرجانات والتحوّل الكبير

بخمسينات وستينات القرن الماضي، لمع نجم فيروز عالمسرح، خصوصاً بمهرجانات بعلبك. الجمهور كان يجي من كل لبنان، ومن برا لبنان كمان، لحتى يسمع صوتا يرتفع قدّام **الأعمدة الرومانية** العريقة. الأغاني اللي قدمتا بهديك المرحلة صارت جزء من الذاكرة اللبنانية: راجعون، سنرجع يوماً، ناطرين، نسم علينا الهوى، سهر الليالي، وبكتب اسمك يا حبيبي.

كانت أغانيا تجمع بين الشعر العميق، اللحن البسيط، والصوت اللي ما بيحتاج قوة ليأثر. قوة فيروز كانت بنعومتا. بأغلب حفلاتا، الجمهور كان يوقف بلا حركة، كأنو عم يسمع صلا.

أسلوبا وتأثيرا

أسلوب فيروز بالغنا بسيط من برا، بس حساس ودقيق. ما بتصرخ، وما بتعمل **استعراض صوتي**، وبتعتمد على الإحساس الواضح بالكلمة واللحن. صوتا فيه لمسة حزن، بس بنفس الوقت في أمل. هالمزيج خلّى أغانيا تعيش عشرات السنين بلا ما تبرد.

اللبنانيين شافوا فيا صورة الوطن، خصوصاً بفترات الحرب. لما البلد كان عم يمر بظروف صعبة، أغانيا كانت متل **ملجأ روحي**. ناس كتير كانت تقول إنو صوت فيروز الوحيد اللي ما اختلفوا عليه اللبنانيين.

السياسة والمسافة الآمنة

رغم إنو فيروز غنت للوطن، وللقدس، وللحب، وللأمل، بس هي شخصياً ما دخلت بالسياسة المباشرة. ما وقفت مع طرف ضد طرف، وما شاركت ببرامج أو خطابات سياسية. كانت تحافظ على **مسافة آمنة**، واعتبرت إنو صوتا لازم يكون لكل الناس، مش لمجموعة معيّنة. هالموقف خلى احترام الناس إلا يكبر أكتر،

رغم إنو أحياناً كان ينفهم غلط.

التكريم والاستمرار

خلال مسيرتا، حصلت فيروز على تكريمات عربية وعالمية كتيرة. أعمالا تُرجمت لعدة لغات، وأسماء كبار الفنانين اعترفوا بتأثيرا علين. حتى مع تقدما بالعمر، بقيت مثال للالتزام **والوقار**. بعد وفاة عاصي وبعد ابتعاد منصور، استمرت بالغنا بالتعاون مع زياد الرحباني، وقدمت لوناً مختلفاً، في جرأة وتجديد.

السنوات الأخيرة والإرث

بالسنوات الأخيرة، قلّ ظهورا، وصارت تعيش حياة هادية، بعيلة صغيرة ومغلقة، وبعيد عن الإعلام. مع هيك، اسما بعدو حاضر كل يوم. أغاني تُسمع بالبيوت، بالمحلات، بالسيارات، وعلى محطات الراديو. وما في صباح بيمرق بلبنان بلا ما ينذكر اسما.

فيروز اليوم مش بس مغنية، هي ذاكرة وطن. أغانيا جمعت ناس من ثقافات ولهجات وبلاد مختلفة، وخليت الشرق يسمع حالو بصوت أجمل.

Comprehension Questions

1. شو كان اسم فيروز الحقيقي؟ و وين خلقت؟

2. كيف كان شكل الحي اللي تربّت فيه ببيروت؟

3. شو اللي خلّى صوتا يلفت الانتباه من هي وصغيرة؟

4. ليش كان الراديو مهم بفترة الحرب العالمية التانية؟

5. مين هو الشخص اللي سمعا لأول مرة بالإذاعة؟ وشو عمل ليدعما؟

6. بأي عمر بلّشت تغنّي بالإذاعة؟

7. كيف صار لقاءا بالأخوين رحباني نقطة تحول بحياتا الفنية؟

8. بأي مهرجانات لمع نجما؟ وشو كانت ميزة هالظهور؟

9. كيف بيوصف النص أسلوب فيروز بالغنى؟

10. ليش اعتبر الناس صوت فيروز ملجأ روحي بفترات الحرب؟

Discussion / Essay Prompts

1. برأيك، في صوت تاني بالعالم العربي قدر يأثر متل فيروز؟ ليش؟

2. كيف بتشوف علاقة الفن بالحرب؟ هل الفن بيلعب دور بتهداية الناس؟

3. بتحس إنو الفنان لازم يبقى بعيد عن السياسة؟ ولا لازم يكون إلو موقف؟ ليش؟

رفيق الحريري

Rafic Hariri was a central figure in Lebanon's modern history, known for his efforts to rebuild the country after the civil war and restore Beirut as a regional center of culture and commerce. Rising from modest beginnings, he became a successful businessman and later a leading political figure with a vision for a stronger, more prosperous Lebanon. His projects in education, infrastructure, and development left a lasting impact on the country and shaped the lives of thousands of people. Even after his tragic assassination, his influence continues to be felt across Lebanon's political and social landscape.

Pre-Reading Questions

1. شو بتعرف عن رفيق الحريري قبل قراية هالنص؟

2. كيف بتتوقع كانت الحياة بلبنان بعد نهاية الحرب الأهلية؟

3. هل بتحس إنو الطموح الشخصي ممكن يغيّر واقع بلد؟ ليش؟

Vocabulary

Read the definitions below. Each one matches a bold word or phrase in the text. Try to guess the terms first, then find them in context as you read. Answers are at the back of the book.

١. الخراب والبقايا بعد الدمار

٢. الطرق، المي، الكهربا، والمباني الأساسية

٣. الفكرة أو الدافع اللي بلش منو كل شي

٤. الوضع السياسي والقوى المسيطرة بالبلد

٥. بسيطة ومن دون رفاهية

٦. خطة أو فكرة كبيرة للمستقبل

٧. شي قوي ومفاجئ بيعمل صدمة

٨. مبالغ كبيرة لازم الدولة تدفعا

٩. مساعدات مالية للتعليم

١٠. مشاكل وعوائق بتوقف التقدم

رفيق الحريري: رجل الإعمار اللي حاول ينهض بلبنان من تحت الركام

الطفولة والبداية

رفيق بهاء الدين الحريري خلق بسنة ١٩٤٤ بمدينة صيدا بلبنان، بعيلة بسيطة. بيو كان مزارع، وإما ربّة بيت. طفولتو كانت **متواضعة**، مليانة تعب وشغل من عمر صغير. درس بمدارس صيدا الرسمية، وكان تلميذ ذكي عندو رغبة كبيرة يغيّر حياتو.

بفترة مراهقتو، اضطر يشتغل ليدعم عيلتو، وكان عندو حلم واضح: إنو يطلع من الفقر ويعمل مستقبل مختلف. وهالحلم كان هو **الشرارة** اللي وصلتو للعالم الكبير.

من صيدا إلى السعودية: بداية الصعود

بسنة ١٩٦٥، ترك لبنان وسافر على السعودية ليشتغل بالتدريس أولاً. بس طموحو ما وقف هون. انتقل لمجال المقاولات، وبلّش من الصفر، خطوة ورا خطوة. بذكا وقدرتو على التواصل، وجرأتو باتخاذ القرارات، قدر يدخل مشاريع كبيرة بالبنية التحتية والإنشاءات.

مع الوقت، صار عندو شركة ضخمة بالمقاولات، وقدر يبني علاقات قوية مع العيلة المالكة بالسعودية. بداية التمانينات، صار الحريري واحد من أبرز رجال الأعمال بالمنطقة، وصار اسمو معروف على مستوى عالمي، خصوصاً بعد ما شارك ببناء مشاريع ضخمة بالسعودية.

العودة إلى لبنان وإعادة الإعمار

بعد نهاية الحرب الأهلية اللبنانية سنة ١٩٩٠، كان لبنان مدمَّر: مباني محروقة،

اقتصاد منهار، وشوارع صارت مجرد ذكرى. رفيق الحريري رجع ومعن **رؤية**: إنو يعيد بناء بيروت، ويرجع للبنان دورو الاقتصادي والثقافي.

بـ١٩٩٢، صار رئيس حكومة، وبلش مشوار طويل من المشاريع: إعادة إعمار وسط بيروت، تطوير **البنية التحتية**، بناء مدارس وجامعات، وإنشاء طرق ومطار جديد.

كان عندو قناعة إنو ما في نهضة بلا استقرار مالي، فحاول يجذب الاستثمارات الخارجية ويعيد الثقة بلبنان. رغم الانتقادات اللي طالتو، خصوصاً بسبب **الديون العالية**، كان واضح إنو عندو طموح ضخم: يشوف لبنان مزدهر متل قبل الحرب، ويمكن أكتر.

العلاقة المعقدة مع السياسة اللبنانية

السياسة بلبنان دايماً صعبة، مليانة تحالفات وتناقضات. الحريري لعب دور أساسي بالمشهد السياسي اللبناني من التسعينات لبداية الألفينات. كان عندو دعم عربي ودولي، وخصوصاً من السعودية وفرنسا، وهيدا ساعدو يكون شخصية مؤثرة.

بس بنفس الوقت، واجه **عراقيل** كبيرة: خلافات مع سياسيين محليين، ضغوط إقليمية، وصراع على دور لبنان بالمنطقة. ومع ذلك، بقي يشتغل، ويبني مدارس، يساعد طلاب، ويؤمن **منح** لآلاف الشباب اللبنانيين ليكملوا دراستن بالجامعات العالمية.

مشروع التعليم والأثر الإنساني

جانب مهم من شخصية الحريري هو الجانب الإنساني. أطلق "مؤسسة الحريري" اللي موّلت تعليم آلاف الطلاب من مختلف الطوايف والمناطق. كتار من المهندسين، الأطبا، الباحثين، والمثقفين اليوم بيقولوا إن الفرصة اللي

أخدوا للدراسة كانت بسببو.

كان عندو إيمان عميق إن التعليم هو الطريق الحقيقي لتغيير المجتمع، وإن مستقبل لبنان لازم يبنى على عقول شاباتو وشبابو.

الاغتيال والصدمة الوطنية

في ١٤ شباط ٢٠٠٥، انفجرت بيروت بخبر هزّ العالم: اغتيال رفيق الحريري بسيارة مفخخة قرب الفندق من سان جورج. الحادث كان **مدوّي**، مش بس بسبب حجمو، بل بسبب تأثيرو السياسي الكبير.

موتو فجّر مرحلة جديدة بلبنان، وفتح الباب لحركة شعبية واسعة، وعمل تغييرات كبيرة **بالخارطة السياسية**.

بس قبل كل شي، كان خسارة إنسانية لشخص كرّس حياتو ليبني بلد، حتى لو أخطأ ببعض الأماكن أو اصطدم بمصالح ناس كتار.

الإرث والتأثير

رفيق الحريري ترك **إرث** كبير ومتناقض أحياناً، بس مؤثّر بلا شك:

• أعاد إعمار جزء كبير من بيروت بعد الحرب
• أعطى آلاف الطلاب فرص تعليمية
• رفع اسم لبنان بالعلاقات الدولية
• حاول يبني مشروع دولة حديثة رغم التعقيدات
• بقي بالنسبة لكتير رمز للنهضة الاقتصادية والاجتماعية

يمكن الناس تختلف برأيا فيه: في ناس بتشوفو بطل بنى بلد، وناس بتشوفة رجل أعمال عندة حسابات سياسية. بس الحقيقة الثابتة إنة ترك بصمة كبيرة بلبنان، بصمة ما زالت واضحة لليوم.

رفيق الحريري كان رجل طموح، حالم، وواقعي بنفس الوقت. أراد لبنان قوي، مزدهر، ومفتوح على العالم. وحتى بعد رحيلة، بصمتة بعدا موجودة بكل شارع من شوارع بيروت.

Comprehension Questions

1. بأي سنة خلق رفيق الحريري وبأي مدينة؟

2. ليش اضطر يشتغل بفترة المراهقة؟

3. شو كان أول عمل إلو بالسعودية؟

4. شو خلا يصير من أبرز رجال الأعمال بالمنطقة؟

5. شو كانت رؤيتو لما رجع على لبنان بعد الحرب؟

6. بأي سنة صار رئيس حكومة؟

7. شو أهم المشاريع اللي عملا بفترة رئاستو؟

8. ليش كانت علاقتو بالسياسة اللبنانية معقدة؟

9. شو هو الجانب الإنساني البارز بشخصية الحريري؟

10. كيف أثر اغتيالو على لبنان؟

Discussion / Essay Prompts

1. بتشوف إنو أغلاط الحريري بتقلّل من إنجازاتو؟ ولا جزء طبيعي من العمل العام؟

2. كيف بتشوف دور رجال الأعمال بإعادة إعمار بلد بعد حرب؟

3. ليش بتعتقد إنو بعض الشخصيات السياسية بتضل مثيرة للجدل حتى بعد موتا؟

حنان الشيخ

Hanan Al-Shaykh is one of Lebanon's most influential contemporary writers, known for her bold exploration of women's lives and the social pressures they face. Her novels often draw on her own experiences growing up in a traditional environment and later living through war, exile, and cultural change. Through honest, vivid storytelling, she gives voice to characters who are rarely heard, highlighting their fears, desires, and struggles. Her work has reached readers around the world, offering a powerful window into Lebanese society and the broader Arab world.

Pre-Reading Questions

١. برأيك، كيف ممكن البيئة المحافظة تأثّر على طريقة كتابة الشخص؟

٢. شو بتعرف عن الحرب الأهلية اللبنانية؟ وكيف بتتوقع إنا أثرت على الكتّاب؟

٣. بتحس الكاتب لازم يحكي عن المواضيع الحساسة حتى لو المجتمع ما بيتقبّل؟ ليش؟

Vocabulary

Read the definitions below. Each one matches a bold word or phrase in the text. Try to guess the terms first, then find them in context as you read. Answers are at the back of the book.

1. البنت اللي بتسمع الكلمة وما بتخالف القوانين

2. تواصل قريب مع الناس وحياتن اليومية

3. شي أولي بيعمل الكاتب منو أفكار أو أعمال

4. طريقة عيش فيا قيود اجتماعية ودينية

5. عيشة برا البلد بشكل طويل عادةً غصب عن الشخص

6. مدرسة الطلاب بيعيشوا فيا مش بس بيدرسوا

7. مكانة قوية ما بتهتز

8. مواضيع المجتمع عادةً ما بيقبل ينحكى عنا

9. ناس حواليك بيراقبوا تصرفاتك وبيحكموا عليا

10. نقلوا الكتاب من لغة للّغة تانية

حنان الشيخ: كتابة تصرخ باسم المرأة والوطن

الطفولة والبداية

حنان الشيخ خلقت ببيروت سنة ١٩٤٥، بعيلة محافظة من الطايفة الشيعية، وعاشت بحيّ راس النبع، واحد من الأحيا التقليدية بالعاصمة. **الجو بالبيت وبالحي كان محافظ**، فيه قوانين واضحة للبنات، وفيه **رقابة اجتماعية** قوية من الأهل والجيران. هالبيئة عملت ضغط عليا من جهة، بس بنفس الوقت صارت هي **المادة الخام** لكتير من رواياتا بعدين، اللي بتحكي عن البنات والنساء تحت عيون المجتمع.

درست وهي صغيرة بمدرسة مخصصة للبنات المسلمات، كان فيا تعليم تقليدي، بيهتم بالدين وبالأخلاق، وبيركّز على فكرة **البنت المطيعة**. بعدين انتقلت على مدرسة أهلية علمانية أكتر، وانفتحت على عالم جديد من الأفكار والكتب. من هديك الفترة، بلشت تكتب لنفسا، متل محاولة للهروب من القيود اللي حاسّتا حواليا.

من بيروت للقاهرة

بسن المراهقة، سافرت على مصر لتكمّل دراستا بالجامعة، ودخلت الكلية الأميركية للبنات بالقاهرة. كانت تجربة مختلفة تماماً عن بيروت المحافظة. سكنت **بمدرسة داخلية**، تعرّفت على بنات من بلاد عربية تانية، وصارت تقرا أدب عالمي وعربي حديث. بهديك الفترة، قرّبت أكتر من عالم الكتابة، وبلشت تشتغل على نصوص أطول، مش بس مقالات أو خواطر قصيرة. وبهديك الفترة كتبت أول رواية إلا، اللي رح تنشر بعد فترة بعنوان "انتحار رجل ميت".

بعد ما خلصت دراستا بالقاهرة سنة ١٩٦٦ تقريباً، رجعت على بيروت واشتغلت بالصحافة، بجرايد ومجلات متل النهار ومجلة الحسناء. الصحافة عطيتا **احتكاك مباشر** مع المجتمع، ومع قصص النساء الحقيقية، من طبقات مختلفة، وهالشي

ساعدا تكوّن لغتا الخاصة بالكتابة.

الكتابة والحرب الأهلية

مع بداية السبعينات، كانت حنان الشيخ صارت اسم معروف ككاتبة وروائية شابة. رواياتا الأولى كانت تلمّح لمواضيع حساسة، بس مع الوقت صارت أكتر جرأة وصراحة، خاصة بطرح حياة المرأة بجسما ورغباتا وخوفا وتمردا. لما اندلعت الحرب الأهلية اللبنانية سنة ١٩٧٥، حياتا اتقلّبت متل حياة كل اللبنانيين. اضطرت تترك بيروت وتعيش فترة بدولة خليجية، وبعدين تنقلت بين كذا بلد، لحد ما استقرّت بلندن بالتمانينات. الحرب ما كانت بس خلفية، كانت جزء من تكوين شخصياتا وأجواء كتبها.

موضوعات جريئة وجدَل

روايات حنان الشيخ معروفة إن فيا موضوعات ناس كتير بتعتبرا **محظور اجتماعية**، خصوصاً بالمجتمعات المحافظة. بتحكي عن الجنس، والزواج، والطلاق، والخيانة، والأمومة، والعنف ضد النساء، وعن علاقة المرأة بجسما وبالمجتمع اللي بيحاول يضبطا كل الوقت. واحدة من أشهر رواياتا "حكاية زهرة"، بتحكي قصة شابة لبنانية مكسورة بين عيلتا وحرب بلدا، وبتقرب كتير من مناطق مسكوت عنا بحياة النساء.

كمان رواية "مسك الغزال" اللي تُرجمت بعنوان "نساء الرمل والمرّ"، بتحط أربع شخصيات نسائية ببلد صحراوي محافظ، وبتفرجي كيف كل واحدة منن بتحاول تلاقي مساحة صغيرة من الحرية داخل مجتمع محافظ. بسبب هالموضوعات، تعرّضت بعض أعمالا للمنع أو صارت صعب تتلاقى ببعض الدول.

من المحلية للعالمية

مع الوقت، طلعت أعمال حنان الشيخ من دائرة القارئ العربي بس، وصارت

تُرجم كتير لغات. روايات متل "حكاية زهرة"، "نساء الرمل والمرّ"، "بريد بيروت" أو "بيروت بلوز"، و"فقط في لندن"، عرّفت القارئ العالمي على وجه مختلف للمدينة العربية، وعلى شخصية نسائية مش نمطية، بتغلط، وبتحب، وبتخاف، وبتثور.

بالسنين الأخيرة، كتبت كمان سيرة حياة أما "حكايتي شرح يطول"، وقدمت إعادة حكي لقصص "ألف ليلة وليلة" بطريقة حديثة. من خلال هالأعمال، صار إلا **موقع ثابت** بين أهم الأصوات الأدبية بالعالم العربي، وصار إلا إرث أدبي واضح ومؤثّر.

الكتابة من المنفى

من لما استقرّت بلندن، حنان الشيخ عاشت تجربة **المنفى** الطويل. بس المنفى عندا مش هروب من المنطقة، بالعكس، صار مرآة بتشوف من خلالا بلدا وحكايات النساء بشكل أوضح. كتير من بطلاتا بيعيشوا بين عالمين، بين بيروت ومدن تانية، بين عيلة محافظة وحياة جديدة، بين لغة البيت ولغة الشارع الأجنبي. هالمسافة عطيتا حرية، بس كمان وجع.

رغم كل التنقلات، بقيت حنان الشيخ قريبة من قضايا النساء، ومن سؤال الحرب والسلام، ومن فكرة كيف الفرد بيقاوم مجتمع محافظ، بالأخص لما يكون هالفرد امرأة بتكتب وبتحكي بصوت عالي.

Comprehension Questions

1. كيف كان الجو بالبيت وبالحي اللي تربّت فيه؟

2. ليش اعتبرت البيئة اللي عاشت فيا مادة خام لكتاباتا؟

3. بأي نوع مدرسة درست بطفولتا؟

4. شو اللي تغيّر بحياتا لما انتقلت على مدرسة علمانية؟

5. شو الإشيا الجديدة اللي تعرّفت عليا خلال إقامتا بالقاهرة؟

6. شو اللي بلّشت تكتبوا بهديك الفترة؟

7. بأي سنة تقريباً خلصت دراستا بالقاهرة؟ وشو عملت بعد ما رجعت على بيروت؟

8. كيف أثرت الحرب الأهلية اللبنانية على حياتا ومسيرتا؟

9. ليش بعض رواياتا تعرّضت للمنع؟

10. كيف بيوصف النص علاقتا بالمنفى وتأثيرو على كتاباتا؟

Discussion / Essay Prompts

1. أي فكرة بالنص حسّيتا قريبة لإلك أو بتشبه واقع ناس بتعرفن؟

2. إذا كنت كاتب أو كاتبة، شو الموضوع الحساس اللي بتحب تكتب عنو؟

3. بتحس إنو العيش برّا البلد (المنفى) بيقوّي صوت الكاتب ولا بيبعّدو عن واقعو؟ ليش؟

فادي الخطيب

Fadi El Khatib is one of Lebanon's greatest basketball legends, known for his strength, determination, and leadership on and off the court. Rising from local playgrounds to international arenas, he became the face of Lebanese basketball during some of its most successful years. His dedication, hard work, and competitive spirit earned him the nickname "The Lebanese Tiger" and inspired young athletes across the region. Today, his legacy lives on not only in his achievements but also in his commitment to developing future generations of players.

Pre-Reading Questions

1. شو بيعنيلك اسم فادي الخطيب؟ بتعرف شي عن مسيرتو بكرة السلّة؟

2. بتتوقع إنو الظروف الصعبة بالبلد بتأثر على اللاعبين؟ كيف؟

3. برأيك، شو اللي بيخلي لاعب يصير رمز لوطن كامل؟

Vocabulary

Read the definitions below. Each one matches a bold word or phrase in the text. Try to guess the terms first, then find them in context as you read. Answers are at the back of the book.

١. أثر قوي ما بينتسى

٢. أهم لاعب بالفريق واللي بيعطي قوة

٣. الأثر اللي تركو بمجال الرياضة وبحياة الناس

٤. المكان اللي بيهرب لعندو من المشاكل

٥. الوصول للشهرة والتميز الرياضي

٦. شغل مش كامل أو بدون إتقان

٧. لاعب مشهور كتير وموهوب

٨. مراكز تدريب بتعلّم اللاعبين

٩. مشاكل وصعوبات قوية واجها

١٠. نشاط كبير دايماً موجود

فادي الخطيب: نمر لبنان وأسطورة كرة السلّة

الطفولة والبدايات

فادي الخطيب خلق سنة ١٩٧٩ بمدينة بيروت بلبنان، وكبر بعيلة بسيطة بتحب الرياضة. من وهو صغير كان عندو **طاقة ما بتخلص**، دايماً يلعب، يركض، ويشارك بكل نشاط رياضي ممكن. بس من وقت حمل طابة السلّة لأول مرة، كان واضح إنّو في شي مختلف. كان طويل، قوي، وعندو خفة حركة مش مألوفة لطفل بعمرو.

مدربينو بالمدرسة لاحظوا موهبتو بسرعة، وبلّش يشارك ببطولات محليّة للناشئين. رغم إنّو كان ببلد مليان مشاكل وحروب، الرياضة كانت **ملجأ الوحيد**، وكان يقول دايماً إنّو "الملعب هو المكان اللي بنسى فيه كل شي".

من الناشئين للنجومية

بانتقالو لفرق الناشئين بفريق الرياضي بيروت، صار اسم فادي يلمع بلبنان. كان يلعب بثقة، وبقوّة، وبجرأة غير عادية. وبعمر ١٨ سنة تقريباً، بلّش يستدعى للمنتخب اللبناني للرجال. هالشي كان إنجاز كبير، خصوصاً بوقت كانت فيه كرة السلّة اللبنانية عم تنهض وتاخد مكان محترم بالمنطقة.

فادي كان سريع التعلّم. يشتغل ساعات طويلة بالتمرين، يهتم باللياقة، ويتابع مباريات كبار اللاعبين بالعالم. وهالالتزام ظهر بسرعة على الملعب.

البطولات الآسيوية وإنجازات المنتخب

أكبر الصفحات بتاريخ فادي الخطيب كانت مع المنتخب اللبناني. من أوائل الألفينيات، صار المنتخب خصم صعب بآسيا، وحقق مراكز متقدمة بعدّة بطولات. فادي كان دايماً **القلب النابض للفريق**: يشجّع، يصرخ، يحارب على كل طابة، ويشيل المنتخب على كتافو بمباريات مصيرية.

بطولة آسيا ٢٠٠١، ٢٠٠٥، ٢٠٠٧، لمع نجمو أكتر وأكتر، واعتُبر من أفضل لاعبي آسيا. الناس صارت تسمّيه "نمر لبنان" بسبب قوّته وارتفاع قفزتو وطريقة لعبو اللي فيا شراسة وإصرار.

وكانت مشاركات لبنان بكأس العالم لكرة السلّة محطات مهمة بتاريخ الرياضة اللبنانية، وفادي كان واحد من أبرز الوجوه اللي قدّمت صورة مشرّقة عن لبنان عالمياً.

المسيرة مع الأندية

لعب فادي الخطيب لعدد كبير من الأندية اللبنانية متل الحكمة والشانفيل والهومنتمن. بكل فريق انتقل عليه، كان يترك **بصمة واضحة**: بطولات، جوايز فردية، وأرقام قياسية.

كمان خاض تجارب احترافية خارج لبنان، خصوصاً بالصين، وهونيك كمان لاقى نجاح كبير. الجمهور الصيني حبّو، والفرق كانت تعتبرو لاعب **سوبر ستار** قادر يغير نتيجة أي مباراة.

الشخصية داخل وخارج الملعب

واحدة من أقوى نقاط فادي كانت شخصيتو. بالملعب كان شرس، بس برا الملعب كان متواضع وقريب من الناس. كان يحب يتواصل مع الجمهور، يتصور مع الأطفال، ويشجعن على الرياضة.

مع إنو عاش إصابات و**تحديات كبيرة**، كان دايماً يرجع أقوى. الإرادة اللي عندو كانت حديث الناس: ما يستسلم، ولا يرضى **بالنصّ نصّ**، دايماً بدّو يكون الأفضل.

الاعتزال والعودة ورحلة الإصرار

أعلن فادي اعتزالو الدولي سنة ٢٠١٧، بس الجماهير ضغطت لدرجة إنو اضطر يرجع ليمثّل لبنان خلال تصفيات كأس العالم ٢٠١٩. هالخطوة أظهرت قدّيش كان محبوب وقدّيش الناس شايفينو رمز ومش مجرد لاعب.

وبعد ما أنهى مسيرتو الطويلة، اتجه للاستثمار بالرياضة وفتح **أكاديميات** تهدف لتدريب جيل جديد من اللاعبين اللبنانيين. كان يؤمن إنّ الرياضة طريقة لإنقاذ الشباب من الضياع وبناء مجتمع أقوى.

إرثو وتأثيرو

فادي الخطيب ما كان مجرد لاعب محترف. كان قدوة. كان رمز لقوة الإرادة، وللاعب اللي حمل وطنو بأصعب الظروف.

إنجازاتو كتيرة:

- هداف تاريخي بالمنتخب اللبناني
- أفضل لاعب بعدة بطولات آسيوية
- مشاركات عالمية مشرّقة
- مسيرة احترافية ناجحة داخل وخارج لبنان
- تأثير كبير على جيل كامل من اللاعبين والشباب

فادي الخطيب كان وما زال أسطورة كرة السلّة اللبنانية. نمر من لبنان، رفع اسم لبنان فوق الملاعب، وترك **إرث رياضي وإنساني** صعب يتكرر.

Comprehension Questions

1. بأي سنة خلق فادي الخطيب وبأي مدينة؟

2. شو كانت صفاتو لما كان صغير؟

3. ليش كانت الرياضة ملجأو الوحيد؟

4. بأي عمر تقريباً انضم للمنتخب اللبناني للرجال؟

5. كيف كان يتميّز فادي بالتمرين والحياة الرياضية؟

6. بأي بطولات آسيوية لمع نجمو؟

7. ليش الناس سمّو نمر لبنان؟

8. شو كانت أهمية مشاركات لبنان بكأس العالم لكرة السلّة؟

9. ليش رجع من الاعتزال ليمثّل لبنان بتصفيات كأس العالم ٢٠١٩؟

10. شو المشاريع اللي اتجه إلا بعد ما أنهى مسيرتو الرياضية؟

Discussion / Essay Prompts

1. برأيك، شو أهم صفات اللاعب اللي بيخلي يصير أسطورة وطنية؟

2. هل بتعتقد إنّو الرياضيين لازم يكونوا قدوة للمجتمع؟ ليش؟

3. لو كنت مدرّب، شو النصيحة اللي كنت تعطيا لفادي لما كان صغير؟

أمل كلوني

Amal Clooney (née Alamuddin) is an internationally respected human rights lawyer known for her sharp legal expertise and her commitment to defending victims of injustice around the world. Born in Lebanon and raised in the United Kingdom, she built her career at some of the most prestigious legal institutions, taking on complex cases involving war crimes, political prisoners, and international law. Her work reflects both professional excellence and a deep belief in accountability and human rights. Today, she stands as a global figure whose achievements continue to inspire people in Lebanon and far beyond.

Pre-Reading Questions

1. شو بيعنيليك اسم أمل كلوني؟ بتعرف شي عن شغلا؟

2. إذا كنت عايش ببلد جديد من عمرك الصغير، بتحس هالشي بيقربك أو بيبعدك عن بلدك الأصلي؟ ليش؟

3. برأيك، المحامي لازم ياخد قضايا صعبة حتى لو بتعرّضو للانتقاد؟ ليش؟

Vocabulary

Read the definitions below. Each one matches a bold word or phrase in the text. Try to guess the terms first, then find them in context as you read. Answers are at the back of the book.

١. أساس قوي بيساعد الشخص يكمّل طريقو

٢. أماكن ومؤتمرات دولية كبيرة

٣. الأثر اللي بتتركو وبيضل بعد نجاحاتا

٤. تعديات على حقوق الأشخاص

٥. روايات الناس اللي تركوا بيوتن بسبب الحرب

٦. عالم الشهرة والتمثيل أو الفن

٧. عيلة بتركّز على العلم والمعرفة

٨. قرارات رسمية لاعتقال أشخاص

٩. كيف الناس بتشوفا وبتفهم شخصيتا

١٠. هجوم أو متابعة من الصحافة والسياسيين

أمل كلوني: محامية حقوق الإنسان
اللي بتمثل وجه لبنان والعالم

الطفولة والبداية

أمل علم الدين، المعروفة اليوم باسم أمل كلوني، خلقت ببيروت سنة ١٩٧٨ **بعيلة مثقفة**. والدا رمزي علم الدين من الدروز، ووالدتا بارعة ميخائيل من الطايفة السنية. بسبب الحرب الأهلية، اضطرت العيلة تترك لبنان بأوائل التمانينات وتستقر ببريطانيا. كبرت أمل بمنطقة هادية بباكينغهامشاير، بس بقيت تسمع **قصص الحرب والتهجير** من أهلا، وهالشي خلق عندا علاقة غريبة بين وطن تركتو بكير وبلد جديد فتّح قدّاما أبواب العلم.

بالمدرسة، كانت طالبة متفوقة، بتحب القراءة والمناقشات. من وهي صغيرة كانت حساسة تجاه الظلم، ودايماً تميل للدفاع عن اللي ما عندن صوت. لما دخلت جامعة أوكسفورد، كان واضح إنّا ما راح تمشي بطريق عادي. تخرّجت بدرجة عالية بالقانون، وبعدين سافرت لنيويورك لتكمّل ماجستير بالقانون، واشتغلت بمكاتب قانونية قوية. هالخبرة العالمية أعطتا **قاعدة صلبة** قبل ما تدخل عالم القانون الدولي.

من بريطانيا للمحافل العالمية

رجعت على لندن وبدأت تمارس القانون بمحاكم عليا. اهتمت خصوصاً بالقانون الدولي وحقوق الإنسان. اشتغلت على قضايا تتعلق بجرايم حرب وحرية الصحافة **وانتهاكات** كبيرة لحقوق الأقليات. وقفت قدّام محاكم دولية، واشتغلت مع لجان تحقيق، ومثّلت ضحايا من مناطق مختلفة من العالم.

تميزت أمل إنا تختار القضايا الصعبة. بالنسبة إلا، القضايا الحساسة هي اللي بتكشف حقيقة القانون، وهي اللي بتختبر قدرة المحامي على التغيير. تدريجياً،

صارت وجه معتمد بمجال حقوق الإنسان، وصار اسما ينذكر بملفات كبيرة كان إلا تأثير دولي.

التحديات والتأثير

الطريق ما كان سهل. أمل واجهت انتقادات بسبب اختيارا تمثل أطراف معينة، وتعرّضت **لضغط إعلامي وسياسي** كبير. مع هيك، كانت تتمسّك بمبدأ بسيط: العدالة للإنسان قبل كل شيء. ببلد متل لبنان عاش الحرب والانقسام، كانت تشوف حالا كواحدة لازم تكون صوت للناس المنسيين. اللبنانيين شافوا قدوة لبنت وصلت للعالمية من دون تترك هويتا أو تخجل بجذورا.

حدث بارز بحياتا المهنية

من أبرز الأحداث اللي لفتت الأنظار لشغلا كان انضماما لفريق قانوني رفع توصية بإصدار **مذكرات توقيف** بحق قادة عالميين بقضايا تتعلق بجرائم حرب وانتهاكات بحق المدنيين. الخطوة كانت جريئة، ورسّخت صورتا كواحدة من المحامين اللي ما بيخافوا من مواجهة القوى الكبيرة. هالملف تحديداً وضعا تحت ضو عالمي أكتر، وفتح نقاشات واسعة حول دور القانون الدولي وحدودو.

الحياة الشخصية والصورة العامة

شهرتا زادت أكتر بعد زواجا من الممثل الأميركي جورج كلوني، لكن الملفت إنا ما سمحت **للحياة الفنية** إنا تغطي على عملا المهني. بالعكس، استغلّت شهرتا لتسليط الضوء على قضايا حقوق الإنسان. أسست مع زوجا مؤسسة تهتم بالعدالة ودعم الصحفيين والنساء حول العالم.

رغم حياتا العالمية، بقيت محافظة على علاقتا بلبنان. ساهمت بمساعدات بعد انفجار بيروت، وقدمت منح تعليمية لطالبات لبنانيات، وكانت دايماً تحكي عن بلدا بحب واحترام. **صورتا العامة** مزيج بين أناقة ظاهرة وشخصية قوية وشغل

جدّي.

اليوم والإرث

اليوم، أمل كلوني واحدة من أهم الأصوات القانونية عالمياً. نجاحا ما كان صدفة، بل نتيجة شغل طويل، وجرأة، وإصرار. بعيون كتير من اللبنانيين، هي مثال للجيل اللي بيقدر يطلع من محنة الحرب ويحمل اسم بلدو بكرامة. **إرثا** مش بس القضايا اللي ربحتا، بل الرسالة اللي بتمثلا: إنو صوت واحد ممكن يعمل فرق، وإنو العدالة ما لازم تكون شعار، بل شغل يومي، شغل بيحتاج صبر وقوة وإيمان.

Comprehension Questions

1. بأي سنة خُلقت أمل علم الدين؟ وبأي حيّ تربّت؟

2. ليش تركت عيلتا لبنان بالأول؟

3. كيف كانت شخصية أمل بالمدرسة؟

4. شو درست بجامعة أوكسفورد؟

5. ليش كانت خبرتا بنيويورك مهمة لبدايتا المهنية؟

6. بأي نوع قضايا ركزت لما رجعت على لندن؟

7. كيف كانت تختار القضايا اللي بتشتغل عليا؟

8. ليش اللبنانيين شافوا قدوة؟

9. شو الحدث البارز اللي زاد شهرتا بمجال القانون؟

10. كيف حافظت على علاقتا بلبنان رغم حياتا العالمية؟

Discussion / Essay Prompts

1. برأيك، هل المحامي لازم يضل محايد، أو لازم يكون عندو موقف أخلاقي؟ ليش؟

2. شو التحديات اللي ممكن يواجها شخص عندو شهرة عالمية بس بيشتغل بقضايا حساسة؟

3. لو كنت محامي، أي نوع قضايا بتحب تترافع فيا؟ وليش؟

جبران خليل جبران

Gibran Khalil Gibran is one of the most influential literary and artistic figures to emerge from Lebanon, best known for his poetic prose and spiritual vision. His writings, including the world-renowned *The Prophet*, explore themes of love, freedom, and the human soul in language that continues to resonate across cultures. Dividing his life between Lebanon and the United States, he developed a unique blend of Eastern and Western influences that shaped his artistic identity. Today, Gibran remains a global symbol of creativity and philosophical insight, with a legacy that bridges nations and generations.

Pre-Reading Questions

1. شو أول شي بيخطر ببالك لما تسمع اسم جبران خليل جبران؟

2. برأيك، كيف بتأثر الهجرة المبكرة على شخصية الكاتب؟

3. شو بتعرف عن أدب المهجر أو الرابطة القلمية؟

Vocabulary

Read the definitions below. Each one matches a bold word or phrase in the text. Try to guess the terms first, then find them in context as you read. Answers are at the back of the book.

1. العيش بعيد عن الوطن لفترة طويلة

2. تلخيص لفكر الشخص ونظرتو للحياة

3. حب قوي تجاه شي معيّن

4. رسومات فيا معاني غير مباشرة

5. عاطفة قوية وصادقة بين الناس

6. عناصر ثقافية وفنية من ثقافتين مختلفتين

7. قوانين أو عادات بيحطا المجتمع على الأفراد

8. كتابات فيا تفكير عميق وشكل قريب للشعر

9. مجموعة كتّاب عندن أفكار مشتركة حول الأدب

10. مفردات وأفكار بتساعد الكاتب يعبّر بوضوح

جبران خليل جبران: شاعر المنفى وصوت الروح

الطفولة والبدايات

جبران خليل جبران خلق ببلدة بشري سنة ١٨٨٣، ببيت فقير بس مليان **محبة**. بشري، بجبالا العالية وغابات الأرز حواليا، تركت أثر عميق بقلبو. كان طفل هادي، خجول، بس خيالو واسع، وكان يحب يرسم على الحيطان والدفاتر الصغيرة.

وضع العيلة ما كان سهل. بيو كان موظّف متواضع وتعرّض لمشاكل مالية وقانونية، وإمو كاملة كانت امرأة قوية، شجاعة، هي اللي حملت البيت على كتافا. سنة ١٨٩٥، لما صار عمر جبران حوالي ١٢ سنة، قررت الأم تاخدو وأخواتو وتهاجر على الولايات المتحدة، تحديداً على بوسطن، لتبلش حياة جديدة بعيد عن الفقر والمشاكل.

الهجرة كانت صدمة لجبران. لغة جديدة، شوارع غريبة، وناس كتير. بس هالتجربة فتحتلو باب ليتعرّف على عالم أوسع، وصارت **المنفى** جزء من تكوين شخصيتو وأعمالو.

من بوسطن لبدايات الفن والأدب

ببوسطن، انتبهوا الأساتذة لموهبتو بالرسم، ونصحو يتسجّل بمعهد فنون. ومع الوقت، صار يرسم **لوحات رمزية**، فيا وجوه حزينة وعيون واسعة، وكانت تلمّح لأسلوب خاص عم يتكوّن عندو. سنة ١٩٠٤، عمل أول معرض فني صغير إلو ببوسطن، وكان هالمعرض بداية ظهور اسمو كرسّام شاب عندو نظرة مختلفة للفن.

بس جبران ما كان بس رسّام. كان عندو **شغف كبير** بالكلمة. تعلّم إنكليزي بسرعة، وصار يكتب أفكار، رسايل، ونصوص قصيرة. سنة ١٩٠٦، نشر أول كتاب

عربي إلو بعنوان "عرائس المروج"، وهو مجموعة قصص فيا رومانسية، تأمل، وفلسفة مبكّرة عن الحياة والإنسان. لغتو بهالكتاب كانت مميزة: نثر فيه موسيقى، وصور شعرية، وأسلوب بيشبه همس الروح أكتر مما بيشبه كتابة تقليدية.

بهالفترة، تعرّف على مثقفين وكتّاب من الجالية السورية واللبنانية بأميركا، وصار جزء من **حركة أدبية** عربية مهاجرة. هالمحيط ساعدو يلاقي صوتو، بين الحنين للوطن والمكان الجديد اللي عم يعيشو.

العودة لبيروت وولادة "جبران الكاتب"

رجع جبران على بيروت سنة ١٨٩٨ لفترة قصيرة ليتعلم بالعربية بشكل أعمق، والتحق بالمدرسة الوطنية ببيروت. بهاي الفترة، كتب قصص ومقالات لفتت الأنظار لقدرة شاب صغير عم يحكي بعمق عن الإنسان، الحرية، الحب، والوجود.

رجعتو لبيروت أعطته **المصطلحات والأدوات** اللي كان ناقصتو ليعبّر بالعربي بكثير من القوة. بعدا عاد لبوسطن، جاهز ليبلّش مشروعو الحقيقي بالكتابة.

الرابطة القلمية وصوت المهجر

جبران انتقل على نيويورك سنة ١٩١١، وهونيك أسس مع ميخائيل نعيمة ونسيب عريضة "الرابطة القلمية"، وهي حركة أدبية جديدة كانت رؤيتا تحديث الأدب العربي وإعطاء الروح مساحة أكبر من الأعراف والشكليات.

كان جبران صوت قوي بالرابطة. لغتو بسيطة بس مش بسيطة، شاعرية بس مش معقّدة، وكان يحكي عن الروح والقلب والحب كأنهن أشخاص من لحم ودم.

كان يؤمن إن الإنسان لازم يتحرر من خوفو ومن **القيود الاجتماعية**، وكانت

كتاباتو مرآة لهالفكرة.

"النبي" والانتشار العالمي

سنة ١٩٢٣، نشر جبران كتابه الأشهر "النبي" باللغة الإنكليزية. الكتاب عبارة عن مجموعة **نصوص شعرية فلسفية** على لسان شخصية حكيم اسمو "المصطفى".

الكتاب نجح بشكل غير مسبوق وصار من أكتر الكتب مبيعاً، ودخل ثقافة العالم كلو، وصار يُقتبس منو بالأعراس، الخطب، الأفلام، والجامعات.

"النبي" ما كان مجرد كتاب، كان **خلاصة رؤية** جبران للعالم: إنو الإنسان، مهما كان أصلو ولغتو ودينو، عندو نفس الأسئلة ونفس الشوق للحب والحرية والمعنى.

الفن، المرض، والسنوات الأخيرة

غير الكتابة، ظل جبران يرسم. لوحاتو فيا **تأثيرات شرقية وغربية**، ووجوه شخصياتو دايماً فيا حزن عميق واتساع بالعينين كأنا شايفة شي أبعد من الواقع.

بآخر سنين حياتو، بلش يعاني من مشاكل صحية بسبب التعب والسهر والكحول. ورغم هيك، بقي يكتب ويرسم.

توفي سنة ١٩٣١ بنيويورك، ورجع جثمانو للبنان ليدفن ببشري حسب وصيتو.

الإرث والتأثير

جبران خليل جبران واحد من أهم الأصوات اللبنانية والعربية والعالمية. كتب عن الإنسان قبل الوطن، وعن الحرية قبل السياسة، وعن الروح قبل الجسد.

أثرو ما زال حي:

- "النبي" ما زال من أشهر الكتب بالعالم
- أدبو المهجري ساهم بتحديث الأدب العربي
- لغتو صارت نموذج للحساسية الشعرية والروحانية
- ولوحاتو جزء مهم من تاريخ الفن الشرقي الحديث

جبران كان شاعر، رسّام، فيلسوف، ومهاجر. بس قبل كل شي، كان إنسان عم يفتّش عن معنى الحياة. ومن مية سنة لليوم، بعدو ناس كتار يلاقوا نفسن بين سطورو وكلامو.

Comprehension Questions

1. وين خلق جبران وبأي سنة؟

2. ليش قررت الأم تاخد جبران وأخواتو وتهاجر؟

3. كيف أثرت الهجرة على شخصية جبران؟

4. شو كان أوّل شي لفت نظر أساتذتو ببوسطن؟

5. بأي سنة عمل أوّل معرض فني لإلو؟

6. شو هو أوّل كتاب عربي نشرو؟ وبأي سنة؟

7. ليش رجع جبران على بيروت سنة ١٨٩٨؟

8. شو الهدف الأساسي من تأسيس الرابطة القلمية؟

9. عن شو بيحكي كتاب النبي؟

10. كيف كانت صحة جبران بسنواتو الأخيرة؟

Discussion / Essay Prompts

1. برأيك، شو سبب إنو كتاب النبي بعدو مشهور لليوم بكل العالم؟

2. هل بتحس إنو حياة المنفى بتقوّي إبداع الكاتب أو بتضعفو؟ ليش؟

3. جبران كان شاعر ورسام وفيلسوف. شو برأيك أصعب موهبة بينن؟

حسن كامل الصبّاح

Hassan Kamel Al-Sabbah is remembered as one of Lebanon's brightest scientific minds, a pioneer whose ideas in electricity and solar energy were far ahead of his time. From his early fascination with light and machines to his groundbreaking research in the United States, he built a reputation as an inventor with a remarkable visionary spirit. His life was cut short at a young age, yet the innovations he left behind continue to inspire engineers and students across the world. Today, Al-Sabbah stands as a symbol of Lebanese talent, creativity, and scientific ambition.

Pre-Reading Questions

1. برأيك، كيف ممكن طفل فضولي يصير عالم كبير؟

2. بتتوقع إنّو السفر للدراسة برّا البلد بيخلق فرص أكبر؟ ليش؟

3. شو بتعرف عن الطاقات المتجددة متل الطاقة الشمسية؟

Vocabulary

Read the definitions below. Each one matches a bold word or phrase in the text. Try to guess the terms first, then find them in context as you read. Answers are at the back of the book.

١. اختبارات صعبة بدا شغل طويل ودقة

٢. الأثر أو الشي اللي بيضل من شخص بعد رحيلو

٣. بداية قوية وفعليّة لمسار مهم

٤. حادث سيارة بيودي للموت

٥. رغبة قوية لمعرفة الإشيا والسؤال عنا

٦. شخص بيعلّم الطلاب وبيعطي دروس

٧. فكرة جديدة كتير بتغيّر المفاهيم السائدة

٨. كتابات شخصية بتنبعت لناس تانيين

٩. مواصلات بتتنقل بسرعة عالية

١٠. وثائق رسمية بتسجّل الاختراع باسم المخترع

حسن كامل الصبّاح: عبقري الكهربا اللي سبق عصرو

الطفولة والبدايات

حسن كامل الصبّاح خلق سنة ١٨٩٤ بمدينة النبطية بجنوب لبنان، ببيت معروف بالعلم والمعرفة. بيو كان شيخ و**معلّم**، ووالدتو مرة قوية ومثقفة، وكانت تشجّعو يقرا ويسأل من وهو صغير.

كبر حسن ببيئة بسيطة بس مليانة **فضول**. كان يحب يفكّ الألعاب ويعيد تركيبا، يراقب البرق والهوا، ويقعد ساعات يتأمل بالضو وبالطبيعة. من عمر صغير، كان واضح إنّو مش طفل عادي، بل عقل علمي عم يتكوّن.

درس بالمدرسة الرسمية وبعدين بمدرسة المقاصد، وكان دايماً الأوّل بصفّو، خصوصاً بالرياضيات. بعدين راح على "الكلّية السورية البروتستانتية" ببيروت، واللي صارت لاحقاً "الجامعة الأميركية". هونيك، توسّع أفقو، وتعرّف على العلوم الحديثة، وبلّشت تظهر عبقريتو الحقيقية بحلّ المسائل الرياضية المعقّدة.

من بيروت لأميركا: بداية التحوّل الكبير

بعد تخرّجو، اشتغل فترة قصيرة بالتدريس، بس شغفو كان أكبر من الصفوف اللبنانية. قرر يسافر على الولايات المتحدة ليكمل دراستو بمجالات الهندسة الكهربائية.

وصل على نيويورك بنهاية العشرينات، والتحق بشركة "جنرال إلكتريك" بمنطقة شينيكتدي. هونيك، صارت **الانطلاقة الحقيقية**. الشركة كانت مركز مهم للبحث العلمي، وفيا كبار المخترعين. بس رغم هيك، بزغ نجم الصبّاح بسرعة.

كان يشتغل ساعات طويلة، ويعمل **تجارب معقّدة**، ويكتب أفكار ويخطط لمشاريع جديدة بجرأة كبيرة. زملاؤو كانوا يستغربوا كيف عقل هالشاب

"الشرقي" أحياناً يسبق تفكيرن بخطوات.

اختراعاتو ورؤيتو المستقبلية

حسن كامل الصبّاح كان سابق عصرو. اشتغل على تطوير الخلايا الشمسية بسنين كان العالم بعدو يعتبر الطاقة الشمسية فكرة مستقبلية بعيدة. كان يؤمن إنّ الشمس رح تكون يوم من الأيام مصدر طاقة نظيفة ومجانية، وإنّو ممكن نشغّل البيوت والسيارات بالطاقة الشمسية.

كمان اشتغل على تطوير المحوّلات الكهربائية، ومحركات جديدة، ودوائر للتحكّم بالطاقة. سجّل **براءات اختراع** بأميركا وبغير دول، وكان عندو خطط لأكتر من **مشروع ثوري**، بينا فكرة "مدينة تشتغل على الكهربا بشكل كامل"، و**وسائل نقل سريعة** تعتمد على أنظمة كهربائية ذكية.

الناس بلشت تسمّي "أديسون الشرق"، وبعض الصحف الأميركية كتبت عنو كواحد من العقول اللي ممكن تغيّر مستقبل التكنولوجيا. كان عندو قدرة يشوف لبعيد، ويتخيّل عالم مختلف تماماً عن العالم اللي عاش فيه.

علاقتو بلبنان وحلمو الكبير

رغم غيابو الطويل عن لبنان، ما نسي بلدو. كان يرسل **رسايل** وينشر مقالات يشجّع فيا الشباب على دراسة العلوم. وكان يحكي للأميركيين بفخر عن لبنان، عن جبالو وناسو.

كان عندو حلم كبير: يرجع على بلدو ويعمل مشروع كهربا ضخم، يربط الجنوب بالشمال، ويوفر طاقة رخيصة للناس. وكان يشوف إنّو نهضة لبنان ممكن تبلش من العلم قبل السياسة.

الحادث المفاجئ والنهاية المؤلمة

بس القدر ما عطاه فرصة يكمل. سنة ١٩٣٥، كان الصبّاح مسافر بسيارتو بولاية كونيتيكت، وتعرّض **لحادث سير مميت.** توفّى عن عمر ٤١ سنة بس.

موتو كان صدمة كبيرة، بلبنان وبأميركا. كتار اعتبروا موتو خسارة عالمية، لأنّو كان بعدو بأول طريقو العلمي، وكان ممكن يقدّم للبشرية أكتر بكتير.

الإرث والتأثير

رغم عمرو القصير، ترك حسن كامل الصبّاح أثر كبير:

- كان من أوائل الباحثين بالطاقة الشمسية بالعالم
- سجّل عشرات براءات الاختراع
- قدّم نظريات بالهندسة الكهربائية بعدا اعتمدتا شركات ومختبرات
- ألهم أجيال من اللبنانيين ليكملوا بطريق العلم

الصبّاح اليوم رمز للعقل اللبناني اللي بيقدر يوصل لأبعد نقطة بالعالم إذا لاقى الفرصة. كان عبقري حقيقي، خيالو واسع، وشغفو بالعلم ما كان إلو حدود. ولو عاش أكتر، كان مسار التكنولوجيا الحديثة يمكن يتغيّر بإيدو.

Comprehension Questions

1. وين خلق حسن كامل الصبّاح وبأي سنة؟

2. شو كان يحب يعمل وهو صغير؟

3. بأي مدارس درس بلبنان؟

4. شو كان يميّزو بالجامعة الأميركية؟

5. ليش قرر يسافر على أميركا؟

6. بأي شركة التحق لما وصل على الولايات المتحدة؟

7. عن شو كانت أكتر اختراعاتو تتركّز؟

8. ليش الناس سمّوه "أديسون الشرق"؟

9. شو كان حلمو الكبير بالنسبة للبنان؟

10. كيف انتهت حياتو، وبأي سنة توفّى؟

Discussion / Essay Prompts

1. برأيك، لو عاش حسن كامل الصبّاح أكتر، كيف كان ممكن يتغيّر عالم التكنولوجيا؟

2. بتحس إنّو المبدع لازم يضل ببلدو أو يسافر ليحقق طموحو؟ ليش؟

3. إذا كنت مهندس أو مخترع، أي نوع اختراع بتحب تعمل؟ وليش؟

شارل مالك

Charles Malik was a prominent Lebanese philosopher, diplomat, and statesman whose work helped shape some of the most important international institutions of the twentieth century. As one of the key drafters of the Universal Declaration of Human Rights, he played a central role in defining global principles of dignity and freedom. His career bridged academia, politics, and diplomacy, reflecting a deep commitment to dialogue and the value of intellectual life. Today, Malik is remembered as a major Lebanese figure whose influence extends far beyond Lebanon's borders.

Pre-Reading Questions

1. شو بتعرف عن الإعلان العالمي لحقوق الإنسان؟ بتعرف مين شارك بصياغتو؟

2. برأيك، كيف بيأثر الفكر الفلسفي على شغل الدبلوماسي؟

3. إذا عاش الشخص طفولتو ببيئة بسيطة، هل هالشي بيمنعو يصير شخصية عالمية؟ ليش؟

Vocabulary

Read the definitions below. Each one matches a bold word or phrase in the text. Try to guess the terms first, then find them in context as you read. Answers are at the back of the book.

١. أفكار متشددة بتقود للعنف أو الإلغاء

٢. أماكن عالمية بيتم فيا اتخاذ قرارات كبيرة

٣. استغلال مجموعات قوية لسلطتا على الضعاف

٤. شخص أفكارو كبيرة بس يمكن صعبة التطبيق

٥. شخص عندو استعداد ليصير فيلسوف

٦. صوت بيمثل فكر راقي واحترام للإنسان

٧. فلسفة بتسأل عن معنى وجود الإنسان وحريتو

٨. كمية كبيرة ومتنوعة من الكتب والمعرفة

٩. مبادئ بتخص كل الناس بكل الدول

١٠. مشاكل وخلافات ناتجة عن الانتماء الديني

شارل مالك: الفيلسوف والدبلوماسي اللي حمل لبنان على المنصّة الدولية

الطفولة والبداية

شارل حبيب مالك خلق ببلدة بطرام بالكورة سنة ١٩٠٦، بعيلة أرثوذكسية بسيطة ومؤمنة بالتعليم والانفتاح. بيو كان طبيب، وإمو ربّة بيت معروفة بحرصا على تربية ولادا على الأخلاق والعلم. الطفولة بشمال لبنان كانت بسيطة، مليانة طبيعة، ومرتبطة بالكنيسة والعادات التقليدية. هالبيئة، مع إنّا هادية، زرعت فيه رغبة يعرف "العالم الأكبر" برّا الجبل والقرى.

كان تلميذ نجيب من صغرو، محب للفلسفة والعلوم. انتقل لبيروت ليتعلم بالمدارس الإرسالية، وهونيك اكتشف **عالم القراءة الواسع**. كان يحب يسأل ويحلّل أكتر ما يحفظ، وهيدا الشي خلّ معلّمينو يشوفوا فيه **مشروع فيلسوف**.

من بيروت لأكبر الجامعات العالمية

بعد ما خلّص مدرسة، دخل الجامعة الأميركية ببيروت، ودرس رياضيات وفلسفة بنفس الوقت، وكان من بين الطلاب اللي يلمعوا بسرعة بسبب فكرن النقدي. بس طموحو ما وقف هون. سافر على ألمانيا بآخر العشرينات ليتخصص أكتر بالفلسفة، وتحديداً **بفكر الوجودية** والمعنى الإنساني. درس بجامعات كبيرة متل هايدلبرغ، وتأثّر بأساتذة كبار متل مارتن هايدغر.

تجربتو بأوروبا ما كانت سهلة. عاش فترة صعود النازية من قريب، وشاف كيف **الفكر المتطرّف** بيقدر يغيّر مصير شعب. هالتجارب حفرت بداخلو قناعة إنو الحرية وكرامة الإنسان لازم يكونوا فوق أي سلطة.

العودة إلى لبنان وبداية المشوار السياسي

رجع شارل مالك على بيروت بداية الأربعينات، وصار يدرّس الفلسفة بالجامعة الأميركية. طلابو كانوا يشوفوا فيه أستاذ مختلف، بيحكي عن الحرية، والوجود، ومسؤولية الفرد، وبيربط الفلسفة بالسياسة والواقع.

ومع بداية استقلال لبنان سنة ١٩٤٣، دخل الحياة الدبلوماسية. تم تعيينو سفير للبنان بالولايات المتحدة، وبعدين سفير بالأمم المتحدة. وجودو بهالموقع سمح إلو ينقل صوت لبنان الصغير لواحدة من أكبر **المنصّات الدولية.**

الإعلان العالمي لحقوق الإنسان

أشهر محطة بحياة شارل مالك هي مشاركتو الأساسية بصياغة الإعلان العالمي لحقوق الإنسان سنة ١٩٤٨. كان عضو باللجنة المصغّرة ومعو Eleanor Roosevelt من أميركا، ورينيه كاسان من فرنسا.

شارل مالك كان الصوت الفلسفي باللجنة: ركّز على إنّو حقوق الإنسان مش بس قوانين، بل **قيم عالمية** لازم تحمي الفرد من ظلم الدولة ومن **تعسّف الجماعات.**

لعب دور مهم بالدفاع عن الحريات الأساسية، وعن مبدأ كرامة الإنسان كمصدر لكل الحقوق. ولما صدر الإعلان، كان لبنان من بين الدول اللي رفعت راسا: بلد صغير شارك بصناعة وثيقة غيّرت تاريخ البشرية.

الدبلوماسية والفكر بمرحلة ما بعد الحرب العالمية

بفترة الخمسينات، صار شارل مالك رئيس الجمعية العامة للأمم المتحدة، وشارك بعدّة مفاوضات كبيرة بعالم السياسة الدولية. كان يحاول دايماً يوازن بين قناعاتو المسيحية الفلسفية وبين واقع السياسة. البعض شافو مفكّر عميق، والبعض اعتبرو **مثالي زيادة**، بس ما حدا شكّ بصدقو ونزاهتو.

رجع على لبنان آخر الخمسينات، وانخرط بالحياة السياسية الداخلية. انتُخب نائب، وتسلّم وزارة الخارجية فترة قصيرة. بس هالمواقع ما كانت تشبهو قد ما كانت الفلسفة والديلوماسية تشبهو. السياسة الداخلية اللبنانية كانت مليانة صراعات طائفية ما انسجمت مع روحو الفكرية.

السنوات الأخيرة والإرث

بعمرو المتقدم، رجع على العمل الفكري وصار يكتب ويحاضر. كتب عن الحرية، العلاقات بين الشرق والغرب، معنى الإنسان، ودور الفرد بخلق عالم أفضل. وبقي مؤمن إنّو لبنان، رغم صغر حجمو، قادر يلعب دور فكري وأخلاقي بالعالم.

توفّي شارل مالك سنة ١٩٨٧، بس إرثو بعدو حاضر:

• مشاركتو بصياغة الإعلان العالمي لحقوق الإنسان
• مساهماتو الفكرية بموضوع الحرية
• تمثيلو للبنان **كصوت حضاري** على الساحة الدولية

شارل مالك كان رجل فكر ورجل دولة، ورجل آمن بالإنسان قبل كل شي. يمكن نختلف مع بعض مواقفو، بس ما فينا ما نعترف إنو كان واحد من أهم العقول اللبنانية اللي تركت أثر عالمي حقيقي.

Comprehension Questions

١. وين خلق شارل مالك وبأي سنة؟

٢. كيف كانت بيئتو العائلية والدينية بطفولتو؟

٣. بأي مواد درس بالجامعة الأميركية ببيروت؟

٤. ليش سافر على ألمانيا؟ وشو الفلسفة اللي ركّز عليا؟

٥. شو شاف شارل مالك بأوروبا بوقت صعود النازية؟

٦. بأي جامعة كان يدرّس بعد ما رجع على بيروت؟

٧. شو المناصب الدبلوماسية اللي استلما بعد استقلال لبنان؟

٨. مين كانوا أعضاء اللجنة المصغّرة لصياغة الإعلان العالمي لحقوق الإنسان؟

٩. شو كان دور شارل مالك الأساسي بهاللجنة؟

١٠. شو المجالات الفكرية اللي كتب عنا بسنواتو الأخيرة؟

Discussion / Essay Prompts

١. برأيك، ممكن فيلسوف يكون دبلوماسي ناجح؟ ولا العالمين ما بينسجموا؟

٢. شو أهمية إنو بلد صغير متل لبنان يشارك بصياغة وثائق عالمية؟

٣. شارل مالك عاش بين الشرق والغرب. برأيك، هالتجربة بتقوّي فكر الإنسان أو بتخلق صراع داخلي؟

نادين لبكي

Nadine Labaki is one of Lebanon's most celebrated filmmakers, known for her ability to blend realism, emotion, and social criticism in powerful cinematic stories. From her early work to her internationally acclaimed films, she has highlighted the daily struggles, hopes, and resilience of people often overlooked in mainstream media. Her bold artistic vision and commitment to portraying authentic Lebanese experiences have earned her recognition at major film festivals around the world. Today, Labaki stands as a leading voice in Arab cinema and a symbol of creative courage and change.

Pre-Reading Questions

١. شو بتعرف عن نادين لبكي أو عن أفلاما قبل ما تقرا هالنص؟

٢. بتحس إنّو القصص الواقعية أقوى، من القصص الخيالية؟ ليش؟

٣. شو بتعرف عن السينما اللبنانية بشكل عام؟

Vocabulary

Read the definitions below. Each one matches a bold word or phrase in the text. Try to guess the terms first, then find them in context as you read. Answers are at the back of the book.

1. أعلى أو أهم نقطة بالمسيرة

2. خلق أسلوب وشخصية فنية واضحة

3. رسالة قوية بتعارض الظلم والفقر

4. طريقة مختلفة عن المتعارف عليا

5. فعاليات كبيرة بتنعرض فيا الأفلام

6. فيا ناس من أكتر من طايفة أو مجموعة

7. قوة بالتصرف أو التعبير بلا خوف

8. مجال دراسة بيجمع بين الصورة والصوت

9. ناس بيمثلوا من دون خبرة سابقة

10. يتنقّل بنظرو ويدقّق بالإشيا حواليه

نادين لبكي: صوت السينما اللبنانية
اللي بيجمع بين الواقع والتمرد

الطفولة والبداية

نادين لبكي خلقت سنة ١٩٧٤ ببلدة بعبدات بجبل لبنان، بعيلة مارونية، بيا كان مهندس وإما ربّة بيت. ترعرعت بلبنان خلال سنوات الحرب الأهلية، فكانت الحياة اليومية مليانة تغييرات، قلق، وتحديات. من صغرا كانت تحب تحكي القصص، تستمع لحكايات خالا اللي كان حكواتي، وتتخيّل أشكالا على الشاشة.

بالمدرسة، كان واضح إنا مش مجرد طالبة عادية: عينيا دايماً **تتجوّل**، تراقب الناس، تحفظ الوجوه وتسجيل تفاصيل صغيرة. وبعد ما تخرّجت من الجامعة اليسوعية ببيروت بدراسة **السمعي-البصري**، بلشت تشتغل بالإعلانات والفيديو كليبات. وكان عندا رغبة قوية تصير مخرجة تحكي بالسينما عن الشارع اللبناني والناس اللي عادةً ما بيظهروا بالأخبار.

الانتقال للسينما وصناعة الهوية

سنة ٢٠٠٧، قدّمت لبكي أول فيلم روائي لا بعنوان «سكر بنات» (Caramel). الفيلم كان كوميدي-درامي، بيدور بأجواء صالون تجميل ببيروت وبيحكي عن خمس نساء بيدوروا حول الحب والخيانة والتقاليد والحرية. الفيلم حقّق نجاح محلي وعالمي، وبيّن إنّو لبنان قادر يعمل سينما بتحكي عن ناسو من دون تصنّع ومن دون مبالغة.

الفيلم التاني «وهلّا لوين؟» سنة ٢٠١١ كان خطوة أكبر. قصتو بتدور بضيعة **مختلطة** فيا مسلم ومسيحي، والنساء فيا عم يحاولوا يمنعوا الرجال من العودة للعنف والحرب. مزجت لبكي الكوميديا بالدراما، وقدرت تقدم صورة رمزية عن لبنان، بلد الأحلام الكبيرة والمشاكل اللي بترجع كل فترة تطلّ.

جرأة الموضوعات والانطلاق العالمي

بس **الذروة الحقيقية** كانت مع فيلما التالت «كفرناحوم» سنة ٢٠١٨، اللي خلى العالم كلو ينتبه إلا. الفيلم بيروي قصة ولد لبناني بلا أدوراق، بيرفع قضية ضد أهلو لأن ولدو بظروف قاسية. الفيلم كان واقعي، مؤلم، ومليان صدق، ولبكي اشتغلت عليه مع **ممثلين غير محترفين** لتقرب قد ما فيا من الحقيقة.

«كفرناحوم» وصل لجوايز عالمية، وترشّح للأوسكار عن فئة أفضل فيلم أجنبي. كانت أول مخرجة عربية بتوصل لهالمستوى. هالفيلم ما كان بس عمل سينمائي، كان **صرخة ضد الفقر**، ضد الظلم، وضد تجاهل الأطفال اللي عايشين بلا حماية.

شخصية لبكي خارج الشاشة

نادين لبكي معروفة بجرأتا، مش بس بإخراجا. بمقابلاتا ولقاءاتا، دايماً بتحكي بصراحة عن الظلم والفساد، وبتصرّ إنّ السينما مش بس فن، بل وسيلة للتغيير. سنة ٢٠١٦ شاركت بترشيحات بلدية بيروت ضمن حملة «بيروت مدينتي»، وكانت تجربتا السياسية محاولة لتقديم **نموذج جديد** للعمل العام.

بحياتا الشخصية، تزوجت من الملحن اللبناني خالد مزنّر سنة ٢٠٠٧، وهنّي بيشكلوا فريق فني متناغم. هو بيتولى الموسيقى، وهي السيناريو والإخراج، وكتير من أعمالن حملت بصمة مشتركة.

الإرث والتأثير

اليوم، نادين لبكي تعتبر واحدة من أهم المخرجات بالعالم العربي. أفلاما دخلت **مهرجانات** كبيرة متل كان، تورونتو، والبندقية، واسما صار مرتبط بسينما إنسانية جريئة، بتقرب من الشارع ومن حياة الناس البسيطة.

إرثا واضح:

• غيّرت صورة المرأة العربية بكاميرا صادقة وقوية
• سلّطت الضوء على الأطفال واللاجئين والفقر كقضايا أساسية
• رفعت مكانة السينما اللبنانية عالمياً
• أثبتت إنّ السينما ممكن تكون صوت للناس قبل ما تكون مجرّد صناعة فنية

نادين لبكي مخرجة، ممثلة، ناشطة، وصانعة تغيير. من ضيعة صغيرة بالجبل،
صارت صوت عالمي، قادرة تواجه الواقع من دون خوف، وتحلم بسينما تعكس
روح لبنان الحقيقي.

Comprehension Questions

١. بأي سنة خلقت نادين لبكي وبأي بلدة؟

٢. كيف أثرت الحرب الأهلية على طفولتا؟

٣. شو درست بالجامعة اليسوعية؟

٤. بأي مجالات بلّشت شغلا قبل الانتقال للسينما؟

٥. عن شو بيحكي فيلم «سكر بنات»؟

٦. شو الموضوع الأساسي بفيلم «وهلّأ لوين؟»؟

٧. ليش فيلم «كفرناحوم» اعتُبر خطوة مهمة عالمياً؟

٨. بأي نشاط سياسي شاركت سنة ٢٠١٦؟

٩. كيف بتتشارك لبكي الشغل الفني مع زوجا خالد مزنّر؟

١٠. شو أنواع القضايا اللي ركّزت عليا بأفلاما؟

Discussion / Essay Prompts

١. برأيك، هل السينما قادرة فعلاً تغيّر مجتمعات؟ ليش أو ليش لأ؟

٢. لو كنت مخرج، عن أي قضية بتحب تعمل فيلم؟

٣. كيف بتشوف العلاقة بين الفن والسياسة من خلال تجربة لبكي؟

بشير الشهابي التاني

Bashir Shihab II was one of the most influential rulers in Lebanon's historical development, known for his strong leadership during a period of major political and social change. Rising to power in the early nineteenth century, he unified different regions and communities under his rule and strengthened Mount Lebanon's autonomy within the Ottoman Empire. His era was marked by both ambitious reforms and complex alliances that shaped the region's future. Today, he remains a key figure for understanding the political land-scape and historical foundations of Lebanon.

Pre-Reading Questions

١. برأيك، ليش كانت التحالفات مهمة بحياة الحكام بلبنان القديم؟

٢. كيف ممكن تكون الخلفية المختلطة عامل قوة لشخص سياسي؟

٣. هل بتتوقع إنو العلاقة بين الجبل والدولة العثمانية كانت سهلة أو معقدة؟ ليش؟

Vocabulary

Read the definitions below. Each one matches a bold word or phrase in the text. Try to guess the terms first, then find them in context as you read. Answers are at the back of the book.

1. العيل اللي عندا السلطة والنفوذ

2. تطويق مكان ومنع الخروج والدخول

3. جمع الضرايب والرسوم من السكان

4. ذكا بالمناورات والتصرفات السياسية

5. رفض وخروج عن السلطة

6. شخص بيعرف يتعامل مع الوضع متل ما هو بلا مثالية

7. قوة وتأثير على القرارات أو الأحداث

8. مباني أو مواقع بتعكس قيمة تاريخية أو فنية

9. منافسة قوية للوصول للحكم أو السيطرة

10. نزاعات وخلافات قوية بين أطراف مختلفة

بشير الشهابي التاني: الأمير اللي غيّر وجه جبل لبنان

الجذور والبداية

بشير الشهابي التاني، المعروف بين الناس باسم "الأمير بشير"، خلِق بسنة ١٧٦٧ ببلدة غزير بكسروان، بعيلة شهابية كانت جزء أساسي من **الطبقة الحاكمة** بجبل لبنان. الشهابيين أصلاً من أصول سنّية جايين من وادي التيم، بس عبر السنين اندمجوا بالمجتمع اللبناني وتبنّوا العيش بين الدروز والمسيحية بنفس الوقت. هالخلفية المختلطة خلّت بشير يفهم تركيبة الجبل وتعقيداتو من وقت كان صغير.

نشأتو كانت بعيلة عندا علاقات واسعة وزعامة سياسية، بس هالشي ما كان ضمانة لشي. جبل لبنان كان مليان **صراعات** بين العيل القوية، خصوصاً بين القيسيين واليمنيين، وبين الإقطاع والدولة العثمانية. من صغرو شاف القتال، الثارات، والتحالفات اللي تتغير حسب المصلحة. هالتجارب صقلت شخصيتو، وخلّتو يصير **سياسي واقعي**، بيعرف إنو القوة وحدا ما بتكفي من دون ذكا.

طريقه للسلطة

ما وصل بشير للحكم بسهولة. بعد وفاة الأمير يوسف الشهابي، كان في صراع كبير على الإمارة. وبشير، اللي كان معروف بجرأتو، دخل **المعركة السياسية** بقوة، وعمل تحالفات مع مشايخ من الدروز والمسيحية. سنة ١٧٨٨، وبعد مفاوضات طويلة وصراعات داخلية، قدر يوصل لإمارة جبل لبنان بدعم من قوى محلية وإقليمية.

من أول يوم حكم فيه، كان بدّو يعمل توازن بين الدروز والمسيحيين، لأنو كان فهم إنّو الجبل ما بيثبُت إلا إذا الكل شعر إنو إلو مكان. ومع الوقت، صار احترام الناس إلو يكبر، حتى خصومو صاروا يعترفوا بإنو أمير يعرف يدير الأزمات.

التحالف مع إبراهيم باشا ومحمد علي

الفصل الأبرز بحياة بشير كان علاقتو بمحمد علي باشا بمصر. وقت قرر محمد علي يوسّع **نفوذو** باتجاه بلاد الشام، شاف ببشير الشهابي شريك مثالي: قائد قوي، بيعرف الجبل، وعندو شرعية بين الناس.

بشير بدورو شاف بهالتحالف فرصة يقوّي سلطتو ويحمي جبل لبنان من العثمانيين. فلما دخل إبراهيم باشا (ابن محمد علي) على الشام، كان بشير هو الداعم الأساسي إلو بالجبل. ساعدو بتأمين الطرق، تجنيد الرجال، وتنظيم الإدارة.

بس هالتحالف كان إلو ثمن. فرض إبراهيم باشا ضرايب عالية على الناس، وجرّد كتير منن من السلاح. هالقرارات سبّبت غضب شعبي، وخلّت بعض القرى **تتمرّد**. وبشير لاقى حالو بموقف صعب: بين شريكو القوي من جهة، وشعبو الغاضب من جهة تانية.

الإصلاحات وبناء الدولة

رغم التوترات، ما في شك إنّو فترة بشير شهدت تغييرات كبيرة. عمل إصلاحات إدارية، نظم **الجباية**، دعم الزراعة، ووسّع الأسواق. وبنى قصر بيت الدين اللي صار اليوم واحد من أهم **المعالم المعمارية** بلبنان.

كان حاكم عندو رؤية: بدّو جبل لبنان يرتاح من الصراعات التقليدية، ويصير إلُو مؤسسات. وبالرغم من إنو الإصلاحات ما كانت كاملة، لكنا كانت خطوة مهمة بتاريخ لبنان السياسي.

السقوط والمنفى

بس التحالف مع محمد علي، اللي أعطى بشير قوة، كان هو نفسو سبب سقوطو. لما رجعت الدولة العثمانية تستعيد سيطرتا على الشام سنة ١٨٤٠

بدعم من إنكلترا والنمسا وروسيا، لاقى بشير حالو بلا حليف.

القوى الأجنبية طلبت منو يتخلى عن إبراهيم باشا، لكنو رفض. النتيجة كانت **حصار** بيت الدين، وبشير اضطر يسلّم حالو.

نُفي على جزيرة مالطا، وبعدين لإسطنبول، وهونيك قضّى آخر أيامو لحد ما مات سنة ١٨٥٠ بعيد عن الجبل اللي حكمو أكتر من نص حياتو.

إرثو وتأثيرو

بشير الشهابي شخصية معقّدة: في ناس بتشوفو بطل أسس لمرحلة جديدة، وفي ناس بتشوفو أمير قوي شدد قبضتو على الجبل. بس ما في خلاف إنو كان لاعب محوري بتاريخ لبنان.

جمع بين **الدهاء السياسي** والشجاعة، بين الطموح الشخصي والرغبة بإصلاح الجبل، بين التحالفات الخارجية وإدارة التوازنات الداخلية.

لولا بشير، كان يمكن جبل لبنان يضل جزيرة منقسمة بين الإقطاعيين. هو حاول — بنجاح وبفشل بنفس الوقت — يصنع "دولة صغيرة" قبل ما تكون فكرة الدولة الحديثة موجودة عند باقي المنطقة.

Comprehension Questions

١. بأي سنة خِلِق بشير الشهابي التاني؟ وبأي بلدة؟

٢. شو أصل عيلتو الشهابية؟ وكيف اندمجوا بالمجتمع اللبناني؟

٣. كيف أثرت الصراعات بجبل لبنان على شخصية بشير؟

٤. شو صار بعد وفاة الأمير يوسف الشهابي؟

٥. ليش كان مهم بالنسبة إلو يعمل توازن بين الدروز والمسيحيين؟

٦. ليش اعتبر محمد علي باشا إنو بشير شريك مناسب؟

٧. شو كانت نتايج القرارات اللي فرضا إبراهيم باشا على الناس؟

٨. أي إصلاحات قام فيا بشير خلال فترة حكمو؟

٩. ليش سقط حكم بشير؟ وشو صار بقصر بيت الدين؟

١٠. وين نفي بشير؟ وكيف كانت نهايتو؟

Discussion / Essay Prompts

١. برأيك، بشير كان قائد إصلاحي ولا حاكم قوي همو السلطة؟ ليش؟

٢. هل التحالف مع قوى خارجية خطوة قوية أو مخاطرة؟ قدّم أمثلة من النص.

٣. لو عشت بهاديك الفترة، بتتوقع كنت تكون مع بشير أو ضدو؟ وضح السبب.

إميلي نصرالله

Emily Nasrallah was a celebrated Lebanese novelist and journalist whose writing captured the beauty of village life, the struggles of war, and the emotional weight of migration. Drawing on her own childhood in southern Lebanon, she created stories filled with warmth, nostalgia, and deep human insight. Her novels often explored the challenges faced by women and families during times of hardship, giving a powerful voice to experiences often overlooked. Today, Nasrallah is remembered as one of Lebanon's most heartfelt literary voices, whose work continues to resonate across generations.

Pre-Reading Questions

١. شو بيعنيلك موضوع الضيعة والهجرة بلبنان؟

٢. شو بتعرف عن حياة النساء بالقرى اللبنانية بمنتصف، القرن الماضي؟

٣. بتتوقع إنو تجربة الدراسة والعمل بالمدينة بتغيّر نظرة الكاتب لأصلو؟ كيف؟

Vocabulary

Read the definitions below. Each one matches a bold word or phrase in the text. Try to guess the terms first, then find them in context as you read. Answers are at the back of the book.

1. أفكار واضحة فيا وعظ أو توجيه

2. ألم حقيقي بيشبه حياة الناس

3. الشي اللي بينطلق منو الكاتب ليعمل أعمالو

4. تواصل قريب مع الناس وحياتن

5. طريقة كلام بسيطة وواقعية متل ما بيحكوا أهل المنطقة

6. عزم وقوة قرار

7. مسؤوليات كبيرة فوق المسؤوليات العادية

8. نقل مباشر لواقع بشوفو الشخص

9. وثّقت مرحلة أو حدث مهم

10. وضوح وبساطة بكتاباتا بدون تعقيد

إميلي نصرالله: صوت المرأة والضيعة والهجرة بلبنان

الطفولة والبدايات

إميلي فارس نصرالله خلقت سنة ١٩٣١ بضيعة الكفير بقضاء مرجعيون، بجنوب لبنان. الضيعة كانت عالية، خضرا، وأهلا عايشين على الزراعة، خصوصاً التبغ. الطفولة بهالمكان كانت بسيطة بس غنية: مدارس صغيرة، صوت الجرس يجمّع الطلاب، وروايح التراب والكروم.

بس بالرغم من جمال الضيعة، كانت الحياة قاسية: شتاء بارد، شغل كتير، ونسوان بيشيلوا مسؤوليات كبيرة. هالتجربة بطبيعتا الحلوة والمرّة، بقيت بالقلب، وصارت **المادة الأساسية** لكتير من قصصا.

إميلي من وهي صغيرة بتحب الكتابة. كانت تسرق وقت من بعد الدرس لتكتب عن أهل الضيعة، عن البنات اللي بيحلموا يكملوا تعليمن، وعن الرجال اللي يتركوا البلد ليهاجروا. مع الوقت، صار صوتا يميّزا، لأنو كان صادق، وعم يحكي **بلهجة الناس** اللي حواليا من دون تصنّع.

من الكفير لبيروت

بعد المدرسة الرسمية، صار لازم تختار: تبقى بالضيعة وتشتغل، أو تسافر لتكمّل تعليما. **إصرارا** خلّاها تختار الطريق الأصعب. راحت على زحلة، وبعدين على الجامعة الأميركية ببيروت، لتدرس الأدب العربي وتبلّش حياة جديدة.

بيروت بهديك الفترة كانت مدينة كبيرة، مليانة أفكار وصراعات سياسية وثقافية. بالنسبة لإميلي، كانت عالم مختلف تماماً عن ضيعتا. ولكن هالتناقض بين الضيعة والمدينة صار مصدر إلهام لإلا، وعلّما تحكي عن تجربتين بنفس الصدق.

اشتغلت صحفية، وكتبت بمجلّات وصحف، وصار عندا **احتكاك مباشر** مع قضايا

المرأة، التعليم، والحياة اليومية بالمدن والقرى. هالمرحلة ساعدتا تنضج كتابتا، وتعطي شكل واضح لصوتا الأدبي.

"طيور أيلول" وبداية المسيرة الأدبية

شهرتا الكبيرة بلّشت مع روايتا الأولى "طيور أيلول" سنة ١٩٦٢، وهي من أهم الأعمال اللي **أرّخت** للحياة الريفية بلبنان وللألم الهجرة. الرواية بتحكي عن ضيعة جنوبية بتودّع شبابا واحد ورا التاني، رجال وصبيان، بيسافروا ليلاقوا بلاد بعيدة فيا فرص أكتر. الأهالي بيبقوا بالضيعة، يتفرّجوا على التلال الفاضية، وعلى البيوت اللي عم تخسر ناسا شوي شوي.

عنوان الرواية مستوحى من طيور شهر أيلول اللي بتهاجر مع أوّل برد، وبتترك خلفا أماكنا الدافية، لتنبش عن حياة تانية. إميلي شبّهت أهل الضيعة بهالطيور: ناس مجبورين يتركوا أرضن رغم تعلّقن فيا.

الرواية فيا حنين كبير، وفيا **وجع واقعي**: الأميات عم ينتظروا رسايل من ولادن، البنات عم يحلموا بسفر أو زواج أو مستقبل مختلف، والضيعة عم تغيّر ملامحا مع كل موجة سفر جديدة.

"طيور أيلول" ما كانت بس رواية، كانت مرآة لوجدان اللبنانيين بهديك الفترة. لاقت نجاح واسع، ترجموا لعدة لغات، وصارت تُدرَّس بالمدارس والجامعات. نجاحا فتح الطريق لقدّام، وكرّس صوت إميلي ككاتبة عندا قدرة تحوّل التفاصيل الصغيرة لحكاية بتمسّ القارئ بالعاطفة والفكر بنفس الوقت.

الحرب الأهلية والكتابة تحت النار

مع بداية الحرب الأهلية سنة ١٩٧٥، بيروت صارت مدينة ممزّقة، كتير من الناس وقفوا عن الكتابة، بس إميلي كمّلت. كتبت عن الخوف، عن ضياع الأولاد بالشوارع، وعن صمت الأميات. كانت تكتب بواقعية مؤلمة، من دون مبالغة ومن

دون تجميل.

رواياتا بهالفترة كانت متل **شهادة حيّة** على يوميات الحرب، وكيف كانت النساء يتحمّلوا **أعباء مضاعفة**: حماية العيلة، تأمين الأكل، ومعالجة جروح الجيران والأولاد.

وكمان رجعت لموضوعا الدايم: الهجرة. لأنو الحرب فتحت موجة جديدة من السفر، وكانت الضيّع تخسر شبابا مرّة تانية.

أدب الأطفال ودور المرأة

غير الروايات للكبار، إميلي كتبت أدب أطفال. كتبا للأطفال مش بسيطة متل ما ممكن نتخيل، بالعكس فيا **رسايل قوية** عن الشجاعة، الأمل، حب الأرض، وتقبّل التغيير.

كمان كانت صوت قوي لقضايا النساء: حق التعليم، حق الاختيار، وحق يكون جزء من الحياة الثقافية. ما كانت ناشطة سياسية بمعنى مباشر، بس كتابتا كانت بحد ذاتا صرخة ضد الظلم.

السنوات الأخيرة والإرث

بآخر سنين حياتا، بقيت قريبةٍ من القرّاء، تكتب، تلتقي بطلاب، وتشارك بندوات. ورغم المرض، بقيت محافظِة على **صفاء أسلوبا**.

توفّت سنة ٢٠١٨، بس أعمالا بعدا بتعيش بقلب القارئ اللبناني والعربي. إرثا واضح:

- روايات عن الضيعة والهجرة بعيون نسائية
- كتابة صادقة وعاطفية
- دفاع مستمر عن حق المرأة بالتعليم والحرية
- مساهمة كبيرة بأدب الأطفال بالعالم العربي

إميلي نصرالله كانت صوت لبنان الحقيقي: صوت الضيعة، وصوت المرأة اللي بتحب وما بتضعف، وصوت الناس اللي كل يوم بيواجهوا الحياة بتفاصيلا الصغيرة والكبيرة.

Comprehension Questions

1. وين خلقت إميلي نصرالله وبأي سنة؟

2. كيف كانت الحياة بالضيعة اللي تربّت فيا؟

3. ليش اختارت تكمّل تعليما وما تبقى بالضيعة؟

4. بأي مدن وجامعات درست؟

5. كيف أثرت بيروت على طريقة كتابتا؟

6. شو أهمية رواية طيور أيلول بمسيرتا الأدبية؟

7. كيف شبّهت الرواية أهل الضيعة بالطيور؟

8. كيف كتبت عن الحرب الأهلية؟

9. شو المواضيع اللي ركّزت عليا بأدب الأطفال؟

10. شو أهم النقاط اللي بتشكّل إرثا الأدبي؟

Discussion / Essay Prompts

1. برأيك، ليش موضوع الهجرة حاضر بقوة بالأدب اللبناني؟

2. شو بتعلمنا قصص الضيعة عن الهوية والانتماء؟

3. كيف بتشوف دور الكتابة بمساندة النساء والمجتمعات الريفية؟

راغب علامة

Ragheb Alama is one of Lebanon's most enduring and beloved singers, known for a career that has spanned decades and influenced audiences across the Arab world. With his warm voice, memorable melodies, and charismatic presence, he became a familiar figure on radio, television, and concert stages. His ability to adapt to changing musical tastes while staying true to his artistic identity helped him remain relevant to multiple generations. Beyond music, his public appearances and humanitarian work have made him a respected cultural icon in Lebanon and beyond.

Pre-Reading Questions

١. برأيك، كيف تأثير الحرب الأهلية ممكن يغيّر مسار حياة فنان؟

٢. بتحس إنّو الأغاني الرومانسية ممكن تعيش أطول من باقي الأنواع؟ ليش؟

٣. شو دور برامج المواهب بتكوين شهرة الفنان اليوم؟

Vocabulary

Read the definitions below. Each one matches a bold word or phrase in the text. Try to guess the terms first, then find them in context as you read. Answers are at the back of the book.

1. أثر واضح ما بينتسى

2. أسلوب فيه مشاعر وحس

3. اللحظة اللي ببلش فيا النجاح

4. الوزن والنغمة السريعة بالغنية

5. تصرفات فيا مساندة وتشجيع

6. خبرة ووعي أكبر بطريقة الغنا

7. روح مرحة وحضور لطيف

8. طريقة حديثة بتناسب الزمن الجديد

9. مجموعة بتقيّم أصوات وأداء المشاركين

10. نوع أو أسلوب موسيقي محدد

راغب علامة: الصوت اللي رافق أجيال وصار جزء من الذاكرة اللبنانية

الطفولة والبداية

راغب علامة، المولود سنة ١٩٦٢ ببيروت، ينتمي لعيلة بسيطة من الجنوب. بيو كان يشتغل بالنجارة، وإمو ربّة بيت تهتم بالولاد. من صغرو، كان راغب مختلف. صوتو كان يلفت الانتباه، وكان يحب يسمع أم كلثوم، عبد الحليم، وصباح. بالمدرسة، كان يشارك بكل الأنشطة الفنية، ويغني بكل حفلة، ومع الوقت صار الكل يعرف إنّو عندو موهبة مش عادية.

لكن الطفولة ما كانت سهلة. لبنان كان بسنين حرب أهلية، والظروف المادية صعبة. رغم كل هالتحديات، حبّو للموسيقى كان أقوى من الخوف والضياع، وكان يهرب من صوت القصف لصوت الغنا. أهلو دعموا حلمو، وشجعوه يكمل بطريق الفن.

الانطلاقة من ستوديو الفن للشهرة العربية

بداية الثمانينات، شارك راغب ببرنامج ستوديو الفن الشهير، وهونيك قدّم أغاني بيّنت قوّة صوتو وتميّز خامتو. ربح المركز الأول، وكانت هاي اللحظة **نقطة الانطلاق**. بعدا مباشرة صار يسجّل أغانيه الخاصة، ويظهر على المسارح بلبنان وبالدول العربية.

صوتو الرومانسي، حضورو على المسرح، وطبيعتو البعيدة عن التصنّع خلّو يدخل قلوب الناس بسرعة. وبفترة قصيرة صار من أبرز الأصوات الجديدة بالعالم العربي.

أعمالو وانتشار أغانيه

من أواخر الثمانينات وطوال التسعينات وبداية الألفينات، صار راغب علامة نجم عربي كامل. أصدر ألبومات ناجحة تركت **بصمة كبيرة**، منا:

• يا ريت، سنة ١٩٨٦، وهو من أوائل أعمالو اللي قدّمتو للجمهور الواسع
• سهّروني الليل، سنة ٢٠٠١، ألبوم **رومانسي** حقّق انتشار كبير
• طب ليه، سنة ٢٠٠٢، ألبوم جمع بين **الإيقاع** والكلمة السهلة
• الحب الكبير، سنة ٢٠٠٤، واحد من أنجح ألبوماتو
• بعشقك، سنة ٢٠٠٨، عمل لاقى نجاح واسع بالعالم العربي
• سنين رايحة، سنة ٢٠١٠، استمرار لمسيرة ناجحة **بأسلوب عصري**
• حبيب ضحكاتي، سنة ٢٠١٤، ألبوم جمع بين **النضج الفني** والتجديد

أغانيه كانت تجمع بين الإحساس والكلمة القريبة من القلب. كان يعرف يختار لحن بيعلق بالذاكرة، وكلمة بتلمس الناس بكل المراحل متل الحب، الفراق، الشوق، الفرح. ومع كل أزمة مر فيا لبنان، كانت أغانيه مساحة نفس للناس، وصار معروف إنو صوتو بيطمن.

الشخصية الفنية وتجديده المستمر

راغب علامة ما التزم **بلون غنائي** واحد. جرّب البوب، والرومانسي، والأغاني الإيقاعية. وقدر يحافظ على نجاحو رغم تغيّر الذوق العام عبر السنين. اشتغل مع أبرز الملحنين، وقدّم نماذج موسيقية جديدة وسهلة الانتشار.

كمان كان عندو حضور قوي على المسرح. عرف يدير الحفلة، ويتفاعل مع الجمهور **بخفة دم** وبحرفية عالية. هالشي خلّاه محبوب عند كل الأجيال، من اللي عرفو بأول مسيرتو للجيل الجديد اللي تابعو من خلال برامج المواهب.

برامج المواهب والوجه التلفزيوني

من أبرز مراحل مسيرتو كانت مشاركتو كعضو **لجنة تحكيم** بآراب آيدول وبعدين بإكس فاكتور. بهالبرامج ظهرت شخصيتو الصريحة والهادية والداعمة للمواهب الشابة.

صار كتير يشوفو الأستاذ اللي بيعرف يقيّم الصوت ويحترم الشخص اللي واقف قدّامو. هالبرامج زادت من شعبيتو على مستوى جديد وعرّفتو لجمهور أوسع.

الجانب الإنساني والمواقف العامة

راغب علامة معروف كمان بنشاطو الإنساني. شارك بحملات بيئية وصحية، ودعم مؤسسات تعليمية وخيرية. وما كان يخاف يعبّر عن رأيو بقضايا اجتماعية وسياسية، يحكي فيا عن الفساد والظروف المعيشية وأمان الناس.

خلال الأزمات اللي مر فيا لبنان، كان يظهر **بمواقف داعمة**، يدعو للتغيير، ويشدّ على إيد المواطن بالطريقة اللي بيعرف فيا يقرّب من الناس. ورغم إنو فنان، ما كان يفصل نفسو عن هموم المجتمع.

الإرث الفني والتأثير

اليوم يعتبر راغب علامة واحد من أهم وأطول الفنانين استمرارية بالعالم العربي. مش بس بسبب صوتو، بل بسبب حضورو، قدرتو يتجدد، وتمسكو بهويتو الفنية.

ترك إرث كبير:
• عشرات الأغاني اللي صارت كلاسيكيات
• جمهور واسع بلبنان وبالعالم العربي
• إسهام مهم بدعم المواهب الجديدة
• حضور قوي بالعمل الإنساني والاجتماعي

راغب علامة صوت رافق وقدّملن أجيال الفرح والحنين بوقت كانوا فيه بأمسّ الحاجة لصوت يخفف عنن. هو فنان لبناني أثبت إنو الفن الحقيقي بيضل، وبيصير جزء من ذاكرة وطن كامل.

Comprehension Questions

1. بأي سنة خلق راغب علامة وبأي مدينة؟

2. بأي برنامج بدأت انطلاقتو الفعلية؟

3. شو كانت نتيجة مشاركتو بستوديو الفن؟

4. شو أنواع الأغاني اللي قدّما بفترة التمانينات والتسعينات والألفينات؟

5. اذكر ٣ ألبومات من أعمالو المذكورة بالنص.

6. ليش كانت أغانيه قريبة من قلوب الناس؟

7. كيف كان حضورو على المسرح؟

8. شو دورو ببرامج آراب آيدول وإكس فاكتور؟

9. بأي أنواع النشاطات الإنسانية شارك؟

10. ليش بيعتبر اليوم من أهم الفنانين استمرارية بالعالم العربي؟

Discussion / Essay Prompts

1. برأيك، ليش بعض الأصوات بترافق الناس لعشرات السنين؟

2. هل بتشوف إنّ الفنان لازم يكون قريب من قضايا الناس؟ ليش؟

3. كيف بتشوف دور الفنان بوقت الأزمات الوطنية؟

Vocabulary Answer Key

Fairuz

6. الأعمدة الرومانية	1. مسافة آمنة
7. استعراض صوتي	2. محبة ودفا
8. مدرسة فنية كاملة	3. نقطة تحول
9. الكورال	4. ملجأ روحي
10. الوقار	5. إرث

Rafic Hariri

6. رؤية	1. الركام
7. مدوّي	2. البنية التحتية
8. الديون العالية	3. الشرارة
9. منح	4. الخارطة السياسية
10. عراقيل	5. متواضعة

Hanan Al-Shaykh

6. مدرسة داخلية	1. البنت المطيعة
7. موقع ثابت	2. احتكاك مباشر
8. محظور اجتماعية	3. المادة الخام
9. رقابة اجتماعية	4. الجو... كان محافظ
10. تُرجمت	5. المنفى

Fadi El Khatib

1. بصمة واضحة
2. القلب النابض للفريق
3. إرث رياضي وإنساني
4. ملجأ الوحيد
5. النجومية

6. النصّ نصّ
7. سوبر ستار
8. أكاديميات
9. تحديات كبيرة
10. طاقة ما بتخلص

Amal Clooney

1. قاعدة صلبة
2. المحافل العالمية
3. إرثًا
4. انتهاكات
5. قصص الحرب والتهجير

6. الحياة الفنية
7. عيلة مثقفة
8. مذكرات توقيف
9. صورتا العامة
10. ضغط إعلامي وسياسي

Gibran Khalil Gibran

1. المنفى
2. خلاصة رؤية
3. شغف كبير
4. لوحات رمزية
5. محبة

6. تأثيرات شرقية وغربية
7. قيود اجتماعية
8. نصوص شعرية فلسفية
9. حركة أدبية
10. مصطلحات وأدوات

Hassan Kamel Al-Sabbah

6. معلّم		1. تجارب معقّدة	
7. مشروع ثوري		2. الإرث	
8. رسايل		3. انطلاقة حقيقية	
9. وسائل نقل سريعة		4. حادث سير مميت	
10. براءات اختراع		5. فضول	

Charles Malik

6. صوت حضاري		1. الفكر المتطرّف	
7. فكر الوجودية		2. المنصّات الدولية	
8. عالم القراءة الواسع		3. تعسّف الجماعات	
9. قيم عالمية		4. مثالي زيادة	
10. صراعات طائفية		5. مشروع فيلسوف	

Nadine Labaki

6. مختلطة		1. الذروة الحقيقية	
7. جرأة		2. صناعة الهوية	
8. السمعي-البصري		3. صرخة ضد الفقر	
9. ممثلين غير محترفين		4. نموذج جديد	
10. يتجوّل		5. مهرجانات	

Bashir Shihab II

6. سياسي واقعي	1. الطبقة الحاكمة
7. نفوذ	2. حصار
8. معالم معمارية	3. الجباية
9. المعركة السياسية	4. دهاء سياسي
10. صراعات	5. تمرّد

Emily Nasrallah

6. إصرارا	1. رسايل قوية
7. أعباء مضاعفة	2. وجع واقعي
8. شهادة حيّة	3. المادة الأساسية
9. أرّخت	4. احتكاك مباشر
10. صفاء أسلوبا	5. لهجة الناس

Ragheb Alama

6. نضج فني	1. بصمة كبيرة
7. خفة دم	2. رومانسي
8. أسلوب عصري	3. نقطة الانطلاق
9. لجنة تحكيم	4. الإيقاع
10. لون غنائي	5. مواقف داعمة

Translations

Fairuz

Fairuz: the voice that brought Lebanon and the Arab world together

Childhood and beginnings

Fairuz's real name is Nihad Haddad. She was born in 1935 in the Zokak el Blat neighborhood in Beirut. The neighborhood was simple, old houses, people who knew each other, and children playing in the street from morning to evening. Her family was from the modest class, and her father was an employee at the printing press that belonged to a Lebanese newspaper. The atmosphere at home was calm, but full of love and warmth. From when she was small, her voice would attract those around her, because it was clean, clear, and there was something that touched you from the first moment.

During the Second World War, the radio was the main means of entertainment for people. Fairuz used to sit and listen to old songs, especially Asmahan and Layla Murad, and imagine herself on the stage. At school, she would participate in the choir, and the teachers noticed that her voice was different from the other boys and girls.

From the radio to the Rahbani brothers

At sixteen years old, Halim El Roumi, the director of the Lebanese radio at the time, heard her, and he decided to give her a chance. He was the one who named her Fairuz, because her voice in his view was like a precious stone. At the radio, she started to sing short and light songs, and she quickly had a small audience that was growing day by day.

In 1951, she met the Rahbani brothers, Assi and Mansour, and this meeting was a turning point in her artistic life. Assi saw in her the voice that could carry a new musical project for Lebanon. From here, the partnership was born that became one of the most famous partnerships in the history of Arabic music. With time, Fairuz married Assi, and the three of them became a complete artistic school.

The festivals and the big shift

In the fifties and sixties of the last century, Fairuz's star shone on the stage, especially at the Baalbek Festivals. The audience would come from all of Lebanon, and from outside Lebanon too, so that they could hear her voice rising in front of the ancient Roman columns. The songs she presented in that period became part of the Lebanese memory: Rajeoun, Sanarjiou Yawman, Natreen, Nassam Alayna el Hawa, Sahar el Layali, and Bektob Ismak Ya Habibi.

Her songs combined deep poetry, simple melody, and a voice that did not need force to have an effect. Fairuz's strength was in her softness. In most of her concerts, the audience would stand without moving, as if they were listening to a prayer.

Her style and her influence

Fairuz's style in singing is simple on the outside, but sensitive and precise. She does not shout, and she does not do vocal showmanship, and she relies on clear feeling in the word and the melody. Her voice has a touch of sadness, but at the same time there is hope. This mixture made her songs live for tens of years without cooling.

The Lebanese saw in her an image of the homeland, especially in periods of war. When the country was going through difficult conditions, her songs were like a spiritual refuge. Many people used to say that Fairuz's voice was the only thing the Lebanese did not disagree on.

Politics and the safe distance

Although Fairuz sang for the homeland, for Jerusalem, for love, and for hope, she herself did not enter direct politics. She did not stand with one side against another, and she did not participate in political programs or speeches. She kept a safe distance, and she considered that her voice had to be for everyone, not for a particular group. This position made people's respect for her grow even more, although sometimes it was misunderstood.

Recognition and continuation

During her career, Fairuz received many Arab and international honors. Her works were translated into several languages, and major artists acknowledged her influence on them. Even as she grew older, she remained an example of commitment and dignity. After the death of Assi and after Mansour stepped back, she continued singing through collaborations with Ziad Rahbani, and she presented a different style, with boldness and renewal.

The later years and the legacy

In recent years, her appearances decreased, and she began to live a calm life, with a small and closed family, and away from the media. Even so, her name is still present every day. Her songs are heard in homes, in shops, in cars, and on radio stations. And there is no morning that passes in Lebanon without her name being mentioned.

Fairuz today is not just a singer, she is the memory of a nation. Her songs brought together people from different cultures, dialects, and countries, and made the East hear itself in a more beautiful voice.

Rafic Hariri

Rafic Hariri: the reconstruction man who tried to lift Lebanon from under the rubble

Childhood and beginnings

Rafic Bahaa El Din Hariri was born in 1944 in the city of Sidon in Lebanon, to a simple family. His father was a farmer, and his mother a housewife. His childhood was modest, full of hardship and work from a young age. He studied in Sidon's public schools, and he was a smart student who had a strong desire to change his life.

During his adolescence, he had to work to support his family, and he had a clear dream: that he would get out of poverty and make a different future. And this dream was the spark that brought him to the big world.

From Sidon to Saudi Arabia: the beginning of the rise

In 1965, he left Lebanon and traveled to Saudi Arabia to work in teaching first. But his ambition did not stop there. He moved to the field of contracting, and he started from zero, step after step. With his intelligence and his ability to communicate, and his boldness in making decisions, he was able to enter major projects in infrastructure and construction.

With time, he came to have a large contracting company, and he was able to build strong relationships with the royal family in Saudi Arabia. At the beginning of the eighties, Hariri became one of the most prominent businessmen in the region, and his name became known worldwide, especially after he participated in building major projects in Saudi Arabia.

The return to Lebanon and the reconstruction

After the end of the Lebanese civil war in 1990, Lebanon was destroyed: burned buildings, a collapsed economy, and streets that had become only a memory. Rafic Hariri returned with a vision: that he would rebuild Beirut, and restore to Lebanon its economic and cultural role.

In 1992, he became prime minister, and he began a long journey of projects: reconstructing downtown Beirut, developing infrastructure, building schools and universities, and establishing roads and a new airport.

He had a conviction that there was no revival without financial stability, so he tried to attract foreign investments and restore confidence in Lebanon. Despite the criticisms directed at him, especially because of the high debts, it was clear that he had a huge ambition: to see Lebanon prosperous like before the war, and maybe more.

The complicated relationship with Lebanese politics

Politics in Lebanon is always difficult, full of alliances and contradictions. Hariri played an essential role in the Lebanese political scene from the nineties to the early two thousands. He had Arab and international support, especially from Saudi Arabia and France, and this helped him become an influential figure.

But at the same time, he faced major obstacles: disagreements with local politicians, regional pressures, and a struggle over Lebanon's role in the region. Even so, he continued to work, to build schools, to help students, and to provide scholarships for thousands of Lebanese youth to complete their studies in global universities.

The education project and the human impact

An important side of Hariri's personality is the human side. He launched the "Hariri Foundation", which funded the education of thousands of students from different sects and regions. Many of today's engineers, doctors, researchers, and intellectuals say that the opportunity they received to study was because of him.

He had a deep belief that education is the true path to changing society, and that the future of Lebanon had to be built on the minds of its young women and men.

The assassination and the national shock

On February 14, 2005, Beirut exploded with news that shook the world: the assassination of Rafic Hariri with a car bomb near the St. Georges Hotel. The incident was resounding, not only because of its size, but because of its major political impact.

His death ignited a new stage in Lebanon, and opened the door to a wide popular movement, and caused major changes in the political landscape.

But before anything, it was a human loss of a person who dedicated his life to building a country, even if he made mistakes in some places or collided with the interests of many people.

The legacy and the impact

Rafic Hariri left a large legacy, sometimes contradictory, but undoubtedly influential:

- He reconstructed a large part of Beirut after the war
- He gave thousands of students educational opportunities
- He raised Lebanon's name in international relations
- He tried to build a modern state project despite the complications

- He remained for many a symbol of economic and social revival

People may differ in their opinions of him: some see him as a hero who built a country, and some see him as a businessman who had political calculations. But the fixed truth is that he left a big mark on Lebanon, a mark that is still clear today.

Rafic Hariri was an ambitious man, a dreamer, and realistic at the same time. He wanted a Lebanon that was strong, prosperous, and open to the world. And even after his departure, his mark is still present in every street of Beirut.

Hanan Al-Shaykh

Hanan al-Sheikh: writing that screams in the name of woman and homeland

Childhood and beginnings

Hanan al-Sheikh was born in Beirut in 1945, to a conservative family from the Shia community, and she lived in the Ras el Nabeh neighborhood, one of the traditional neighborhoods of the capital. The atmosphere at home and in the neighborhood was conservative, with clear rules for girls, and with strong social supervision from the parents and the neighbors. This environment put pressure on her from one side, but at the same time it became the raw material for many of her later novels, which speak about girls and women under the eyes of society.

When she was small, she studied in a school designated for Muslim girls, where the education was traditional, focused on religion and morals, and concentrated on the idea of the obedient girl. Then she moved to a more secular private school, and she opened up to a new world of ideas and books. From that period, she started to write for herself, like an attempt to escape from the restrictions she felt around her.

From Beirut to Cairo

As a teenager, she traveled to Egypt to continue her studies at the university, and she entered the American College for Girls in Cairo. It was an experience completely different from conservative Beirut. She lived in a boarding school, met girls from other Arab countries, and started reading modern world and Arab literature. In that period, she grew closer to the world of writing, and she started to work on longer texts, not just articles or short reflections. And in that period she wrote her first novel, which would be published later under the title "The Suicide of a Dead Man".

After she finished her studies in Cairo around 1966, she returned to Beirut and worked in journalism, in newspapers and magazines like An Nahar and Al-Hasnaa Magazine. Journalism gave her direct contact with society, and with the real stories of women, from different classes, and this helped her form her own language in writing.

Writing and the civil war

With the beginning of the seventies, Hanan al-Sheikh had become a known name as a young writer and novelist. Her early novels hinted at sensitive subjects, but with time they became more bold and frank, especially in presenting the life of woman in her body, her desires, her fear, and her rebellion. When the Lebanese civil war broke out in 1975, her life was turned upside down like the life of all the Lebanese. She had to leave Beirut and live for a period in a Gulf country, and then she moved between several countries, until she settled in London in the eighties. The war was not only a background, it was part of the formation of her characters and the atmosphere of her books.

Bold themes and controversy

Hanan al-Sheikh's novels are known for containing themes that many people consider social taboos, especially in conservative societies. They speak about sex, marriage, divorce, betrayal, motherhood, violence against women, and about the woman's relationship with her body and with the society that tries to control her all the time. One of her most famous novels, "The Story of Zahra", tells the story of a young Lebanese woman broken between her family and the war of her country, and it comes very close to areas unspoken in the lives of women.

Also the novel "Musk al-Ghazal", which was translated under the title "Women of Sand and Myrrh", places four female characters in a conservative desert country, and shows how each one of them tries to find a small space of freedom inside a conservative society. Because of these themes, some of her works were subjected to banning or became difficult to find in some countries.

From local to global

With time, Hanan al-Sheikh's works went beyond the circle of the Arab reader only, and they began to be translated into many languages. Novels like "The Story of Zahra", "Women of Sand and Myrrh", "Beirut Mail" or "Beirut Blues", and "Only in London", introduced the global reader to a different face of the Arab city, and to a female character that is not stereotypical, who makes mistakes, loves, fears, and revolts.

In recent years, she also wrote the life story of her mother, "The Story I Am Too Long to Tell", and she presented a retelling of the "One Thousand and One Nights" stories in a modern way. Through these works, she came to have a fixed place among the most important literary voices in the Arab world, and she came to have a clear and influential literary legacy.

Writing from exile

Since she settled in London, Hanan al-Sheikh has lived the experience of long exile. But exile for her is not an escape from the region, on the contrary, it became a mirror through which she sees her country and the stories of women more clearly. Many of her heroines live between two worlds, between Beirut and other cities, between a conservative family and a new life, between the language of home and the language of the foreign street. This distance gave her freedom, but also pain.

Despite all the moving around, Hanan al-Sheikh remained close to women's issues, and to the question of war and peace, and to the idea of how the individual resists a conservative society, especially when this individual is a woman who writes and speaks out loud.

Fadi El Khatib

Fadi El Khatib: Lebanon's tiger and a basketball legend

Childhood and beginnings

Fadi El Khatib was born in 1979 in the city of Beirut in Lebanon, and he grew up in a simple family that loved sports. From when he was small, he had energy that did not end, always playing, running, and participating in every possible sports activity. But from the moment he held a basketball for the first time, it was clear that there was something different. He was tall, strong, and had a lightness of movement not usual for a child his age.

His school coaches noticed his talent quickly, and he started to participate in local junior tournaments. Even though he was in a country full of problems and wars, sports were his only refuge, and he used to always say that "the court is the place where I forget everything".

From juniors to stardom

With his move to the junior teams of Riyadi Beirut, Fadi's name began to shine in Lebanon. He played with confidence, with strength, and with unusual boldness. And at about 18 years old, he began to be called up to the Lebanese men's national team. This was a major achievement, especially at a time when Lebanese basketball was rising and taking a respectable place in the region.

Fadi learned quickly. He worked long hours in training, took care of his fitness, and followed the matches of the world's top players. And this commitment appeared quickly on the court.

The Asian championships and the national team's achievements

The biggest pages in Fadi El Khatib's history were with the Lebanese national team. From the early two thousands, the national team became a tough opponent in Asia, and it achieved high rankings in several tournaments. Fadi was always the beating heart of the team: encouraging, shouting, fighting for every ball, and carrying the national team on his shoulders in decisive matches.

In the Asia Championship in 2001, 2005, and 2007, his star shone more and more, and he was considered one of the best players in Asia. People started to call him "Lebanon's Tiger" because of his strength, his jump height, and his way of playing that had ferocity and determination.

And Lebanon's appearances in the Basketball World Cup were important milestones in the history of Lebanese sports, and Fadi was one of the most prominent faces who presented an honorable image of Lebanon internationally.

The career with clubs

Fadi El Khatib played for a large number of Lebanese clubs like Hekmeh, Champville, and Homenetmen. In every team he moved to, he left a clear mark: championships, individual awards, and record numbers.

He also had professional experiences outside Lebanon, especially in China, and there too he found great success. The Chinese fans loved him, and the teams considered him a superstar player capable of changing the result of any match.

The personality on and off the court

One of Fadi's strongest points was his personality. On the court he was fierce, but off the court he was humble and close to people. He liked to interact with the fans, take photos with children, and encourage them in sports.

Even though he lived through injuries and major challenges, he always came back stronger. The will he had was the talk of the people: he did not give up, and he did not accept half measures, he always wanted to be the best.

Retirement, return, and the journey of determination

Fadi announced his international retirement in 2017, but the fans pressured him to the point that he had to return to represent Lebanon during the qualifiers for the 2019 World Cup. This step showed how loved he was and how much people saw him as a symbol and not just a player.

And after he finished his long career, he turned to investment in sports and opened academies aimed at training a new generation of Lebanese players. He believed that sports were a way to save youth from being lost and to build a stronger society.

His legacy and influence

Fadi El Khatib was not just a professional player. He was a role model. He was a symbol of willpower, and of a player who carried his country in the hardest conditions.

His achievements are many:

- A historic top scorer with the Lebanese national team

- Best player in several Asian championships

- Honorable international appearances

- A successful professional career inside and outside Lebanon

- A major influence on a whole generation of players and youth

Fadi El Khatib was and still is a legend of Lebanese basketball. A tiger from Lebanon, he raised Lebanon's name above the courts, and he left a sports and human legacy that is difficult to repeat.

Amal Clooney

Amal Clooney: the human rights lawyer who represents the face of Lebanon and the world

Childhood and beginnings

Amal Alamuddin, known today as Amal Clooney, was born in Beirut in 1978 to an educated family. Her father Ramzi Alamuddin is from the Druze community, and her mother Baria Mikhael is from the Sunni community. Because of the civil war, the family had to leave Lebanon in the early eighties and settle in Britain. Amal grew up in a quiet area in Buckinghamshire, but she kept hearing stories of war and displacement from her parents, and this created in her a strange relationship between a homeland she left early and a new country that opened the doors of knowledge before her.

At school, she was an excellent student, who loved reading and discussions. From when she was small, she was sensitive toward injustice, and she always tended to defend those who had no voice. When she entered Oxford University, it was clear that she was not going to follow an ordinary path. She graduated with a high degree in law, and then she traveled to New York to complete a master's in law, and she worked in strong law firms. This global experience gave her a solid base before she entered the world of international law.

From Britain to global forums

She returned to London and began practicing law in high courts. She was especially interested in international law and human rights. She worked on cases related to war crimes, freedom of the press, and major violations of minority rights. She stood before international courts, worked with investigation committees, and represented victims from different regions of the world.

Amal distinguished herself by choosing the difficult cases. For her, the sensitive cases are the ones that reveal the truth of the law, and they are the ones that test the lawyer's ability to make change. Gradually, she became a trusted face in the field of human rights, and her name started to be mentioned in major files where she had an international impact.

The challenges and the influence

The path was not easy. Amal faced criticism because of her choice to represent certain parties, and she was subjected to major media and political pressure. Even so, she held on to a simple principle: justice for the human being before anything. In a country like Lebanon that lived through war and division, she saw herself as someone who had to be a voice for forgotten people. The Lebanese saw a role model in a girl who reached global recognition without leaving her identity or being ashamed of her roots.

A major event in her professional life

One of the most notable events that drew attention to her work was her joining a legal team that issued a recommendation to issue arrest warrants for global leaders in cases related to war crimes and violations against civilians. The step was bold, and it cemented her image as one of the lawyers who do not fear facing powerful forces. This file in particular placed her under greater global light, and opened wide discussions about the role of international law and its limits.

Personal life and public image

Her fame increased further after her marriage to the American actor George Clooney, but what was notable was that she did not allow the artistic life to overshadow her professional work. On the contrary, she used her fame to shine light on human rights issues. She founded with her husband a foundation concerned with justice and supporting journalists and women around the world.

Despite her global life, she remained committed to her connection with Lebanon. She contributed with aid after the Beirut explosion, provided educational scholarships to Lebanese female students, and she always spoke about her country with love and respect. Her public image is a mixture of visible elegance and a strong personality and serious work.

Today and the legacy

Today, Amal Clooney is one of the most important legal voices globally. Her success was not a coincidence, but the result of long work, boldness, and determination. In the eyes of many Lebanese, she is an example for a generation that can rise from the hardship of war and carry the name of its country with dignity. Her legacy is not only the cases she won, but the message she represents: that one voice can make a difference, and that justice must not be a slogan, but daily work, work that needs patience, strength, and faith.

Gibran Khalil Gibran

Gibran Khalil Gibran: the poet of exile and the voice of the soul

Childhood and beginnings

Gibran Khalil Gibran was born in the town of Bsharri in 1883, in a poor house but full of love. Bsharri, with its high mountains and its cedar forests around it, left a deep impact in his heart. He was a quiet, shy child, but with a wide imagination, and he loved to draw on walls and in small notebooks.

The family's situation was not easy. His father was a modest employee who faced financial and legal problems, and his mother Kamile was a strong, courageous woman who carried the house on her shoulders. In 1895, when Gibran was about 12 years old, the mother decided to take him and his siblings and emigrate to the United States, specifically to Boston, to start a new life far from poverty and problems.

The emigration was a shock for Gibran. A new language, strange streets, and many people. But this experience opened a door for him to get to know a wider world, and exile became part of the formation of his personality and his works.

From Boston to the beginnings of art and literature

In Boston, the teachers noticed his talent in drawing, and they advised him to enroll in an art institute. With time, he began drawing symbolic paintings, with sad faces and wide eyes, and they hinted at a special style forming in him. In 1904, he held his first small art exhibition in Boston, and this exhibition was the beginning of the appearance of his name as a young painter who had a different vision of art.

But Gibran was not only a painter. He had a great passion for the word. He learned English quickly, and he began to write thoughts, letters, and short texts. In 1906, he published his first Arabic book titled "Nymphs of the Valley", which is a collection of stories containing romance, reflection, and early philosophy about life and the human being. His language in this book was distinctive: prose with music, poetic images, and a style that resembled the whisper of the soul more than traditional writing.

In this period, he met intellectuals and writers from the Syrian and Lebanese community in America, and he became part of an Arab immigrant literary movement. This environment helped him find his voice, between longing for the homeland and the new place he was living.

The return to Beirut and the birth of "Gibran the writer"

Gibran returned to Beirut in 1898 for a short period to learn Arabic more deeply, and he joined the National School in Beirut. In this period, he wrote stories and articles that drew attention to the ability of a young man speaking with depth about the human being, freedom, love, and existence.

His return to Beirut gave him the terms and the tools he needed to express himself in Arabic with much greater strength. After that he returned to Boston, ready to begin his true project in writing.

The Pen League and the voice of the diaspora

Gibran moved to New York in 1911, and there he founded with Mikhail Naimy and Nasib Arida the "Pen League", a new literary movement whose vision was to modernize Arabic literature and give the spirit more space than conventions and formalities.

Gibran was a strong voice in the league. His language was simple but not simple, poetic but not complicated, and he spoke about the soul, the heart, and love as if they were people made of flesh and blood.

He believed that the human being must free himself from his fear and from social restrictions, and his writings were a mirror of this idea.

"The Prophet" and global spread

In 1923, Gibran published his most famous book, "The Prophet", in English. The book is a collection of poetic philosophical texts in the voice of a wise character named "Almustafa".

The book succeeded in an unprecedented way and became one of the best-selling books, and it entered the culture of the whole world, and it came to be quoted at weddings, speeches, films, and universities.

"The Prophet" was not just a book, it was the summary of Gibran's vision of the world: that the human being, whatever his origin, language, or religion, has the same questions and the same longing for love, freedom, and meaning.

Art, illness, and the later years

Besides writing, Gibran continued to paint. His paintings had Eastern and Western influences, and the faces of his characters always had deep sadness and wide eyes as if they were seeing something beyond reality.

In the last years of his life, he began to suffer from health problems because of exhaustion, staying up late, and alcohol. Even so, he continued to write and paint.

He died in 1931 in New York, and his body was returned to Lebanon to be buried in Bsharri according to his will.

The legacy and the influence

Gibran Khalil Gibran is one of the most important Lebanese, Arab, and global voices. He wrote about the human being before the homeland, about freedom before politics, and about the soul before the body.

His influence is still alive:

- "The Prophet" is still one of the most famous books in the world
- His immigrant literature contributed to modernizing Arabic literature
- His language became a model of poetic sensitivity and spirituality
- And his paintings are an important part of the history of modern Eastern art

Gibran was a poet, painter, philosopher, and immigrant. But before anything, he was a human being searching for the meaning of life. And from a hundred years until today, many people still find themselves between his lines and his words.

Hassan Kamel Al-Sabbah

Hassan Kamel Al-Sabbah: the electricity genius who was ahead of his time

Childhood and beginnings

Hassan Kamel Al-Sabbah was born in 1894 in the city of Nabatieh in southern Lebanon, in a house known for knowledge and learning. His father was a sheikh and a teacher, and his mother was a strong and educated woman who encouraged him to read and ask questions from when he was small.

Hassan grew up in a simple environment but full of curiosity. He loved to take apart toys and put them back together, to observe lightning and wind, and to sit for hours contemplating light and nature. From a young age, it was clear that he was not an ordinary child, but a scientific mind in formation.

He studied in the public school and then at the Maqasid School, and he was always the top of his class, especially in mathematics. Then he went to the "Syrian Protestant College" in Beirut, which later became the "American University". There, his horizons widened, he got to know modern sciences, and his true genius began to appear in solving complex mathematical problems.

From Beirut to America: the beginning of the great transformation

After he graduated, he worked for a short period in teaching, but his passion was greater than the Lebanese classrooms. He decided to travel to the United States to complete his studies in the fields of electrical engineering.

He arrived in New York at the end of the twenties, and he joined the "General Electric" company in the Schenectady area. There, the real beginning happened.

The company was an important center for scientific research, and it had major inventors. But even so, Al-Sabbah's star rose quickly.

He worked long hours, conducted complex experiments, wrote ideas, and planned new projects with great boldness. His colleagues were surprised how the mind of this "Eastern" young man sometimes preceded their thinking by steps.

His inventions and his futuristic vision

Hassan Kamel Al-Sabbah was ahead of his time. He worked on developing solar cells in years when the world still considered solar energy a distant futuristic idea. He believed that the sun would one day be a source of clean and free energy, and that it would be possible to run homes and cars on solar power.

He also worked on developing electrical transformers, new engines, and circuits for power control. He registered patents in America and other countries, and he had plans for more than one revolutionary project, among them the idea of "a city that runs entirely on electricity", and fast transportation methods that rely on smart electrical systems.

People began to call him "the Edison of the East", and some American newspapers wrote about him as one of the minds that could change the future of technology. He had the ability to see far ahead, and to imagine a world completely different from the one he lived in.

His relationship with Lebanon and his big dream

Despite his long absence from Lebanon, he did not forget his country. He used to send letters and publish articles encouraging youth to study sciences. And he spoke to Americans with pride about Lebanon, about its mountains and its people.

He had a big dream: to return to his country and create a major electricity project, connecting the south to the north, and providing cheap energy for people. And he saw that Lebanon's revival could start from science before politics.

The sudden accident and the painful end

But fate did not give him the chance to continue. In 1935, Al-Sabbah was traveling by car in the state of Connecticut, and he was involved in a fatal traffic accident. He died at only 41 years old.

His death was a major shock, in Lebanon and in America. Many considered his death a global loss, because he was still at the beginning of his scientific path, and he could have contributed much more to humanity.

The legacy and the influence

Despite his short life, Hassan Kamel Al-Sabbah left a major impact:

- He was one of the earliest researchers in solar energy in the world

- He registered dozens of patents
- He presented theories in electrical engineering that companies and laboratories later adopted
- He inspired generations of Lebanese to continue on the path of science

Al-Sabbah today is a symbol of the Lebanese mind that can reach the farthest point in the world if it finds the opportunity. He was a true genius, with a wide imagination, and his passion for science had no limits. And if he had lived longer, the course of modern technology might have changed at his hands.

Charles Malik

Charles Malik: the philosopher and diplomat who carried Lebanon onto the international platform

Childhood and beginnings

Charles Habib Malik was born in the village of Btarām in Koura in 1906, to a simple Orthodox family that believed in education and openness. His father was a doctor, and his mother a homemaker known for her care in raising her children on ethics and learning. Childhood in northern Lebanon was simple, full of nature, and tied to the church and traditional customs. This environment, although calm, planted in him a desire to know "the larger world" outside the mountain and the villages.

He was an excellent student from when he was young, fond of philosophy and sciences. He moved to Beirut to study in missionary schools, and there he discovered the wide world of reading. He liked to ask and analyze more than to memorize, and this made his teachers see in him the making of a philosopher.

From Beirut to the world's great universities

After he finished school, he entered the American University of Beirut, and he studied mathematics and philosophy at the same time, and he was among the students who quickly stood out because of their critical thinking. But his ambition did not stop there. He traveled to Germany in the late twenties to specialize further in philosophy, specifically in existential thought and human meaning. He studied at major universities like Heidelberg, and he was influenced by major professors like Martin Heidegger.

His experience in Europe was not easy. He lived through the rise of Nazism up close, and he saw how extremist thought could change the fate of a people. These experiences engraved in him the conviction that freedom and human dignity must be above any authority.

The return to Lebanon and the beginning of the political path

Charles Malik returned to Beirut in the early forties, and he began teaching philosophy at the American University. His students saw in him a different professor, someone who spoke about freedom, existence, and the responsibility of the individual, and who linked philosophy with politics and reality.

With the beginning of Lebanon's independence in 1943, he entered diplomatic life. He was appointed Lebanon's ambassador to the United States, and then ambassador to the United Nations. His presence in this position allowed him to carry the voice of small Lebanon to one of the largest international platforms.

The Universal Declaration of Human Rights

The most famous milestone in Charles Malik's life is his essential participation in drafting the Universal Declaration of Human Rights in 1948. He was a member of the small committee along with Eleanor Roosevelt from America and René Cassin from France.

Charles Malik was the philosophical voice in the committee: he focused on the idea that human rights are not just laws, but universal values that must protect the individual from the injustice of the state and the abuse of groups.

He played an important role in defending basic freedoms, and in the principle that human dignity is the source of all rights. And when the declaration was issued, Lebanon was among the countries that raised its head: a small country had participated in creating a document that changed human history.

Diplomacy and thought in the period after the Second World War

In the fifties, Charles Malik became president of the General Assembly of the United Nations, and he participated in several major negotiations in the world of international politics. He always tried to balance his Christian philosophical convictions with the reality of politics. Some saw him as a deep thinker, and some considered him too idealistic, but no one doubted his honesty and integrity.

He returned to Lebanon in the late fifties, and he became involved in internal political life. He was elected a member of parliament, and he took charge of the Ministry of Foreign Affairs for a short period. But these positions did not resemble him as much as philosophy and diplomacy did. Lebanese internal politics were full of sectarian conflicts that did not match his intellectual spirit.

The later years and the legacy

In his advanced age, he returned to intellectual work and began to write and lecture. He wrote about freedom, the relations between East and West, the meaning of the human being, and the role of the individual in creating a better world. And he remained convinced that Lebanon, despite its small size, was capable of playing an intellectual and moral role in the world.

Charles Malik died in 1987, but his legacy is still present:

- His participation in drafting the Universal Declaration of Human Rights
- His intellectual contributions on the subject of freedom
- His representing Lebanon as a civilized voice on the international stage

Charles Malik was a man of thought and a man of state, and a man who believed in the human being before anything. We may disagree with some of his positions, but we cannot fail to acknowledge that he was one of the most important Lebanese minds who left a true global impact.

Nadine Labaki

Nadine Labaki: the voice of Lebanese cinema that brings together reality and rebellion

Childhood and beginnings

Nadine Labaki was born in 1974 in the town of Baabdat in Mount Lebanon, to a Maronite family. Her father was an engineer and her mother a homemaker. She grew up in Lebanon during the years of the civil war, so daily life was full of changes, anxiety, and challenges. From when she was small, she loved telling stories, listening to the tales of her uncle who was a storyteller, and imagining shapes on the screen.

At school, it was clear that she was not just an ordinary student: her eyes always roamed, observing people, memorizing faces, and recording small details. And after she graduated from Saint Joseph University in Beirut with a degree in audiovisual studies, she began working in advertising and music videos. And she had a strong desire to become a director who would speak in cinema about the Lebanese street and the people who usually do not appear in the news.

The move to cinema and the creation of identity

In 2007, Labaki presented her first feature film, titled Caramel. The film was a comedy-drama set in the atmosphere of a beauty salon in Beirut, and it tells the story of five women who revolve around love, betrayal, traditions, and freedom. The film achieved local and international success, and it showed that Lebanon was capable of making cinema that speaks about its people without artificiality and without exaggeration.

Her second film, Where Do We Go Now?, in 2011 was a bigger step. Its story takes place in a mixed village with Muslims and Christians, and the women there are trying to prevent the men from returning to violence and war. Labaki blended comedy with drama, and she was able to present a symbolic image of Lebanon, a country of big dreams and problems that keep returning every once in a while.

Bold themes and global rise

But the true peak was with her third film, Capernaum, in 2018, which made the whole world notice her. The film tells the story of a Lebanese child without papers who files a lawsuit against his parents because they gave birth to him in harsh conditions. The film was realistic, painful, and full of truth, and Labaki worked on it with nonprofessional actors to get as close as possible to reality.

Capernaum reached global awards and was nominated for the Oscar for Best Foreign Film. She was the first Arab female director to reach this level. This film was not just a cinematic work, it was a cry against poverty, against injustice, and against ignoring the children who live without protection.

Labaki's personality off screen

Nadine Labaki is known for her boldness, not only in her directing. In her interviews and appearances, she always speaks frankly about injustice and corruption, and she insists that cinema is not only an art but also a means of change. In 2016, she participated in the Beirut municipal elections within the "Beirut Madinati" campaign, and her political experience was an attempt to present a new model of public work.

In her personal life, she married the Lebanese composer Khaled Mouzanar in 2007, and they form a harmonious artistic team. He takes charge of the music, and she of the script and directing, and many of their works carry a shared imprint.

The legacy and the influence

Today, Nadine Labaki is considered one of the most important directors in the Arab world. Her films entered major festivals such as Cannes, Toronto, and Venice, and her name became associated with bold human cinema that comes close to the street and to the lives of ordinary people.

Her legacy is clear:

- She changed the image of the Arab woman with a camera that is honest and strong
- She shed light on children, refugees, and poverty as essential issues
- She raised the status of Lebanese cinema globally
- She proved that cinema can be a voice for people before being merely an artistic industry

Nadine Labaki is a director, actress, activist, and maker of change. From a small mountain village, she became a global voice, capable of facing reality without fear, and dreaming of a cinema that reflects the true spirit of Lebanon.

Bashir Shihab II

Bashir Shihabi II: the prince who changed the face of Mount Lebanon

Roots and beginnings

Bashir Shihabi II, known among people as "Prince Bashir", was born in 1767 in the town of Ghazir in Keserwan, to a Shihabi family that was a fundamental part of the ruling class in Mount Lebanon. The Shihabis were originally of Sunni origin coming from Wadi al-Taym, but over the years they integrated into Lebanese society and adopted living among Druze and Christians at the same time. This mixed background made Bashir understand the composition of the mountain and its complexities from when he was young.

His upbringing was in a family with wide connections and political leadership, but this was not a guarantee of anything. Mount Lebanon was full of conflicts between powerful families, especially between the Qaysites and the Yemenites, and between the feudal system and the Ottoman state. From his childhood he saw fighting, vendettas, and alliances that changed according to interest. These experiences refined his personality and made him a realistic politician who knew that power alone was not enough without intelligence.

His path to power

Bashir did not reach power easily. After the death of Prince Yusuf Shihabi, there was a major struggle over the emirate. And Bashir, who was known for his boldness, entered the political battle strongly, and he made alliances with sheikhs from the Druze and the Christians. In 1788, after long negotiations and internal conflicts, he was able to reach the Emirate of Mount Lebanon with the support of local and regional powers.

From the first day he ruled, he wanted to create balance between Druze and Christians, because he understood that the mountain would not be stable unless everyone felt they had a place. And with time, people's respect for him grew, and even his opponents began to acknowledge that he was a prince who knew how to manage crises.

The alliance with Ibrahim Pasha and Muhammad Ali

The most prominent chapter in Bashir's life was his relationship with Muhammad Ali Pasha in Egypt. When Muhammad Ali decided to expand his influence toward the Levant, he saw in Bashir Shihabi an ideal partner: a strong leader who knew the mountain and who had legitimacy among the people.

Bashir in turn saw in this alliance an opportunity to strengthen his authority and protect Mount Lebanon from the Ottomans. So when Ibrahim Pasha (the son of Muhammad Ali) entered the Levant, Bashir was his main supporter in the mountain. He helped him secure the roads, recruit men, and organize administration.

But this alliance had a price. Ibrahim Pasha imposed high taxes on the people and disarmed many of them. These decisions caused popular anger and made some villages rebel. And Bashir found himself in a difficult position: between his powerful partner on one side and his angry people on the other.

Reforms and state-building

Despite the tensions, there is no doubt that Bashir's period witnessed major changes. He carried out administrative reforms, organized taxation, supported agriculture, and expanded the markets. And he built Beit ed-Dine Palace, which today is one of the most important architectural landmarks in Lebanon.

He was a ruler with a vision: he wanted Mount Lebanon to rest from traditional conflicts and to have institutions. And although the reforms were not complete, they were an important step in the political history of Lebanon.

The fall and exile

But the alliance with Muhammad Ali, which gave Bashir power, was the same thing that caused his fall. When the Ottoman state regained its control over the Levant in 1840 with the support of England, Austria, and Russia, Bashir found himself without an ally.

The foreign powers asked him to abandon Ibrahim Pasha, but he refused. The result was the siege of Beit ed-Dine, and Bashir was forced to surrender himself.

He was exiled to the island of Malta, and then to Istanbul, and there he spent his last days until he died in 1850, far from the mountain he had ruled for more than half his life.

His legacy and influence

Bashir Shihabi is a complex character: some people see him as a hero who laid the foundation for a new stage, and some see him as a strong prince who tightened his grip on the mountain. But there is no disagreement that he was a pivotal player in the history of Lebanon.

He combined political cunning and courage, personal ambition and the desire to reform the mountain, external alliances and the management of internal balances.

If it were not for Bashir, Mount Lebanon might have remained an island divided among feudal lords. He tried, with success and failure at the same time, to create a "small state" before the idea of the modern state existed in the rest of the region.

Emily Nasrallah

Emily Nasrallah: the voice of woman, village, and migration in Lebanon

Childhood and beginnings

Emily Fares Nasrallah was born in 1931 in the village of Al-Kfeir in the Marjayoun district in southern Lebanon. The village was high, green, and its people lived on agriculture, especially tobacco. Childhood in this place was simple but rich: small schools, the sound of the bell gathering students, and the smells of soil and vineyards.

But despite the beauty of the village, life was harsh: a cold winter, a lot of work, and women carrying large responsibilities. This experience, with its sweet and bitter sides, stayed in the heart, and became the essential material for many of her stories.

Emily from when she was small loved writing. She used to steal time after lessons to write about the people of the village, about the girls who dreamed of continuing their education, and about the men who left the country to migrate. With time, her voice became distinguished, because it was honest and was speaking in the dialect of the people around her without artificiality.

From Al-Kfeir to Beirut

After public school, she had to choose: stay in the village and work, or travel to continue her education. Her determination made her choose the harder path. She went to Zahle, and then to the American University of Beirut, to study Arabic literature and begin a new life.

Beirut in that period was a big city, full of ideas and political and cultural conflicts. For Emily, it was a world completely different from her village. But this contrast between the village and the city became a source of inspiration for her, and it taught her to speak about two experiences with the same honesty.

She worked as a journalist, and she wrote in magazines and newspapers, and she had direct contact with issues concerning women, education, and daily life in cities and villages. This stage helped her mature as a writer and gave a clear shape to her literary voice.

"September Birds" and the beginning of the literary career

Her great fame began with her first novel, September Birds, in 1962, which is among the most important works that chronicled rural life in Lebanon and the pain of migration. The novel tells the story of a southern village that bids farewell to its youth one after the other, men and boys, who travel to find distant lands with more opportunities. The families remain in the village, watching the empty hills and the houses that are slowly losing their people.

The title of the novel is inspired by the birds of the month of September that migrate with the first cold, leaving behind their warm places to search for another life. Emily compared the people of the village to these birds: people forced to leave their land despite their attachment to it.

The novel contains great longing, and realistic pain: mothers waiting for letters from their sons, girls dreaming of travel or marriage or a different future, and the village changing its features with every new wave of travel.

September Birds was not just a novel, it was a mirror of the Lebanese spirit in that period. It found wide success, was translated into several languages, and came to be taught in schools and universities. Its success opened the road ahead and established Emily's voice as a writer with the ability to turn small details into a story that touches the reader emotionally and intellectually at the same time.

The civil war and writing under fire

With the beginning of the civil war in 1975, Beirut became a torn city. Many people stopped writing, but Emily continued. She wrote about fear, about children lost in the streets, and about the silence of mothers. She wrote with painful realism, without exaggeration and without beautification.

Her novels in this period were like a living testimony to the daily life of the war, and how women bore double burdens: protecting the family, providing food, and tending to the wounds of neighbors and children.

And she also returned to her constant theme: migration. Because the war opened a new wave of travel, and the villages lost their youth once again.

Children's literature and the role of women

Besides novels for adults, Emily wrote children's literature. Her books for children were not simple as one might imagine, rather they contained strong messages about courage, hope, love of land, and accepting change.

She was also a strong voice for women's causes: the right to education, the right to choose, and the right to be part of cultural life. She was not a political activist in the direct sense, but her writing itself was a cry against injustice.

The final years and the legacy

In the last years of her life, she remained close to readers, writing, meeting students, and participating in seminars. And despite illness, she remained preserving the clarity of her style.

She died in 2018, but her works still live in the hearts of Lebanese and Arab readers. Her legacy is clear:

- Novels about the village and migration through women's eyes
- Honest and emotional writing

- Continuous defense of women's right to education and freedom
- A major contribution to children's literature in the Arab world

Emily Nasrallah was the true voice of Lebanon: the voice of the village, the voice of the woman who loves and does not weaken, and the voice of the people who every day face life with its small and large details.

Ragheb Alama

Ragheb Alama: the voice that accompanied generations and became part of Lebanese memory

Childhood and beginnings

Ragheb Alama, born in 1962 in Beirut, belongs to a simple family from the south. His father worked in carpentry, and his mother was a homemaker who took care of the children. From when he was small, Ragheb was different. His voice attracted attention, and he loved listening to Umm Kulthum, Abdel Halim, and Sabah. At school, he took part in all artistic activities, and he sang at every event, and with time everyone came to know that he had an extraordinary talent.

But childhood was not easy. Lebanon was in the years of civil war, and financial conditions were difficult. Despite all these challenges, his love for music was stronger than fear and loss, and he would escape from the sound of shelling to the sound of singing. His family supported his dream and encouraged him to continue on the artistic path.

The start from Studio El Fan to Arab fame

In the early eighties, Ragheb participated in the famous program Studio El Fan, and there he presented songs that showed the strength of his voice and the distinction of his vocal quality. He won first place, and that moment was the starting point. After that, he immediately began recording his own songs and appearing on stages in Lebanon and in Arab countries.

His romantic voice, his presence on stage, and his unpretentious nature made him enter people's hearts quickly. And in a short period he became one of the most prominent new voices in the Arab world.

His works and the spread of his songs

From the late eighties throughout the nineties and the beginning of the two thousands, Ragheb Alama became a complete Arab star. He released successful albums that left a major mark, among them:

- Ya Reit, in 1986, one of his earliest works that introduced him to the wide public
- Saharouni El Leil, in 2001, a romantic album that achieved great reach

- Tab Leih, in 2002, an album that combined rhythm with simple lyrics
- El Hob El Kbir, in 2004, one of his most successful albums
- Baashaqik, in 2008, a work that found wide success in the Arab world
- Sneen Rayha, in 2010, a continuation of a successful career in a modern style
- Habeeb Dahkati, in 2014, an album that combined artistic maturity and renewal

His songs combined emotion with words close to the heart. He knew how to choose a melody that stuck in memory, and lyrics that touched people through all stages like love, separation, longing, and joy. And with every crisis Lebanon went through, his songs were a breathing space for the people, and it became known that his voice reassured.

His artistic personality and his continuous renewal

Ragheb Alama did not commit himself to one musical style. He tried pop, romantic, and rhythmic songs. And he was able to maintain his success despite changes in public taste through the years. He worked with the most prominent composers, and he presented new musical models that were easy to spread.

He also had a strong presence on stage. He knew how to run a concert and interact with the audience with lightness and high professionalism. This made him loved by all generations, from those who knew him at the beginning of his career to the new generation who followed him through talent shows.

Talent shows and the television persona

One of the most prominent phases of his career was his participation as a judge on Arab Idol and then on The X Factor. In these programs, his frank, calm, and supportive personality toward young talents appeared.

People came to see him as the teacher who knows how to evaluate the voice and respect the person standing before him. These programs increased his popularity on a new level and introduced him to a wider audience.

The humanitarian side and public stances

Ragheb Alama is also known for his humanitarian activity. He took part in environmental and health campaigns, and he supported educational and charitable institutions. And he did not fear expressing his opinion on social and political issues, speaking about corruption, living conditions, and people's safety.

During the crises that Lebanon went through, he appeared with supportive stances, calling for change, and strengthening the hand of the citizen in the way he knew how to come close to people. And although he was an artist, he did not separate himself from the concerns of society.

The artistic legacy and influence

Today Ragheb Alama is considered one of the most important and longest-lasting artists in the Arab world. Not only because of his voice, but because of his presence, his ability to renew himself, and his commitment to his artistic identity.

He left a major legacy:

- Dozens of songs that became classics
- A wide audience in Lebanon and the Arab world
- An important contribution to supporting new talents
- A strong presence in humanitarian and social work

Ragheb Alama is a voice that accompanied generations and gave them joy and longing at a time when they were in great need of a voice that would ease their burdens. He is a Lebanese artist who proved that true art remains, and becomes part of the memory of an entire nation.

lingualism

Visit our website for information on current and upcoming titles and free language learning resources.

www.lingualism.com